THE PIONEER

1850 – 1. ..

DAVID HOLLETT
WITH A FOREWORD BY
NICK BARRETT
Chief Executive, The Ramblers' Association

THE PIONEER RAMBLERS
1850-1940

DAVID HOLLETT

First published in March 2002

Printed by MFP Design & Print, Manchester

Published by the North Wales Area of the Ramblers' Association

All profits from the sale of the first edition of this publication are
being donated by the author to the funds of the North Wales Area of
the Ramblers' Association

A CIP catalogue record for this book is available from the British Library

ISBN 1-901184-54-4

BY THE SAME AUTHOR

From Cumberland to Cape Horn	Fairplay Publications, London, 1984
Fast Passage to Australia	Fairplay Publications, London, 1986
Merseyside and the 19th Century Emigrant Trade to Australia	Wirral Metropolitan Borough Council, 1987
Men of Iron. The Story of Cammell Laird Shipbuilders 1828 - 1991	Wirral Metropolitan Borough Council, 1992
The Alabama Affair	1st Edition: Sigma Leisure, Wilmslow, 1993 2nd Edition: Avid Publications, Wirral, 2002
The Conquest of the Niger by Land & Sea	Heaton Publishing, Abergavenny, April, 1995
Passage to the New World	Heaton Publishing, Abergavenny, May, 1995
Passage from India to El Dorado	Associated University Presses, Cranbury, New Jersey, 1999
The Clwydian Way Long Distance Trail	The Ramblers' Association, 2000

ACKNOWLEDGEMENTS

The author would like to thank the following institutions, organisations and individuals for their invaluable assistance.

VERA HOLLETT
My wife, Vera Hollett, for her invaluable support throughout this long project

BOB READ
My son-in-law, Bob Read, for preparing the illustrations for publication

CHARLOTTE WILLIAMS (FORMERLY PRAGER)
Publications & Information Manager, RA London, for information and support

DONALD ROOKSBY
Of the Ramblers' Association, North Wales Area, for proof reading the draft copy

---

The Ramblers' Association, London
The Ramblers' Association, Merseyside and West Cheshire Area
The Youth Hostel Association
The Pennine Way Association
The Long Distance Walkers Association
The Open Spaces Society
The Forest Ramblers
The Manchester Evening News
Liverpool City Libraries
Birkenhead Central Library
Liverpool University Library
Sheffield Central Libraries and Archives

The British Library, London,
The British Newspaper Library, Colindale
Manchester Central Library
The Mitchell Library, Glasgow
The Highland Council Library Support Unit, Inverness
London Metropolitan Archives
The Countryman
The Guardian and The Observer
The Derbyshire Advertiser

ILLUSTRATIONS

The Ramblers' Association, for illustrations on pages: 95. 97. 98.
99. 100. 101. 115. 126. 128.
The Youth Hostel Association for illustrations on pages: 102. 107.
108.
Chris Sainty, Secretary, The Pennine Way Association, for the
illustration on page 114, taken from his own collection.

CONTENTS

Chapters   PAGE

1	The Battle of Glen Tilt	1
2	Heading for the Highlands	17
3	Winans versus Murdo Mackrae	28
4	James Bryce and the Access Bills	49
5	The Commons Preservation Society	61
6	The Sunday Tramps	73
7	Pioneering Rambling Clubs – 1874 –1900	84
8	The Sheffield Clarion Ramblers	98
9	Long Distance Walking	106
10	The Lake District and the 'Lakers'	118
11	Some early 20th Century Rambling Clubs	132
12	The Nineteen Thirties	148
13	The Youth Hostel Association	160
14	The Ramblers' Association	170
15	Kinder Scout and other Access Rallies	182
	References	203
	Index	212

LIST OF ILLUSTRATIONS

Page

Front   Genteel Ramblers, 1886
Back   Ramblers ascending Ben Nevis, 1881
4   Deer stalking in the Highlands: 'A sketch in Glen Tilt.'
5   Highland Deerstalking: 'By George! Missed again.'
10   Scene from the burlesque recently performed at Glen Tilt
16   Tourists on board a Highland steamer, 1871
19   A tour in Scotland: On board the Iona, 1873
21   The 'hotel' and observatory on Ben Nevis, 1885
22   The Major and his entourage climbing Ben Nevis, 1881
29   Interior of a crofter's hut, Isle of Lewis, 1888
35   The Prince of Wales in the Highlands in 1880
43   Land reform being discussed at a village pub in 1892
46   Reading the 'Riot Act' to crofters, Isle of Lewis, 1888
46   Crofters of Lewis in combat with police and marines, 1888
48   The gunboat Jackal, at Loch Luirbost, 1888
51   Views in the Vale of Rannoch, Scotland, in 1884
53   James Bryce, MP for South Aberdeen
58   Heading out to a Royal Hunt in the Highlands in 1880
63   Sketches on Hampstead Heath, 1871
64   Epping Forest – view from High Beech – 1884
65   Commons Preservation. Sketch of Barnes Common, 1877
68   'No Thoroughfare' 'Trespassers will be prosecuted'
71   A picnic at Burnham Beeches, near Slough, in 1879
72   The Advantages of our suburbs
75   Leslie Steven and party ascending the Rothhorn
77   Arrested for trespassing. The hazards of rambling in 1884
80   Kitchen of the 'Walnut Tree Inn' Adlington in 1885
83   A 'Fogbow' as seen from the Matterhorn
86   Leaving Home, 1888
89   Birkenhead Photographic Society at Burton in the 1920's

92   With the Hop Pickers in Kent, 1886

93   Yorkshire Ramblers' Club Territory, North Yorkshire, 1885

102   The Penrhyn slate quarry, Bethesda, 1892

109   William Gale walking 1,500 miles in a thousand hours

110   Finish of the Great Walking-Match, Islington, 1878

112   Weston's Temperance walk of 5,000 miles in 100 days

124   Aira Force

125   Launch of 'Lady of the Lake', on Windermere, 1845

126   Harriet Martineau

128   'Lady of the Lake Loquiter'

130   The steam vessel Gondola on Coniston, 1860

135   'Trespassers will be prosecuted'

138   A Day's Sketching with the Field Naturalist, 1887

139   Equestrians v. Pedestrians

140   Sights to be seen by pioneer ramblers in the country

143   Some Incidents of a Walking Tour, 1885

147   A day trip in a 'Charabanc' in the 1920's

149   L.M.S. Walking Tour Booklet

152   Wayfaring Holidays in Scotland

153   "A Comradeship Holiday is the Holiday for you" (1932)

154   "F.H.A. Holidays are Great"

156   A typical C.H.A. advertisement of the inter-war period

158   From the cover of Y.H.A. "Rucksack" February 1936

159   A Pioneer Rambler – Mr. T. Arthur Leonard in 1932

167   The 'Waysmeet' Hostel, All Saints' Lane, Canterbury

169   The Glen Nevis Youth Hostel

178   Tom Stephenson, Barbara Castle, Mike Harding and others

180   Top Withens in Bronte Country

181   Outline map of the proposed Pennine Way prepared in 1938

182   Veteran rambler Benny Rothman, at Holm village, 1990

184   Grouse driving in Derbyshire

186   Plaque commemorating the Kinder Trespass of 1932

188   Lane leading down to the centre of Hayfield

194   A Head Keeper standing by his substantial cottage

198 G.B.H. Ward of Sheffield addressing a Winnats Pass
     Demonstration
199 Federation Demonstration, Thurstaston Hill, 1927
202 "How to make a Socialist"

FOREWORD

One of the most interesting things about the history of the rambling movement in Britain is the extent to which it reflects social and political change. The history told by David Hollett in these pages amply illustrates this and along the way it also tells some extremely entertaining stories about the early rambling groups, their activities, beliefs and sheer eccentricity.

In the 19th century rambling was a hobby indulged in by those who didn't need to earn their income. These people were close to the land owning classes and therefore did little to rock the boat: thus for example the terrible clearances in the Scottish Highlands went relatively unchallenged. Only when the industrial revolution created sufficient filth and poverty of life in the cities did the people demand to be allowed to walk freely in the countryside.

The intellectual ramblers of the early 19th Century did not enjoy sharing the beauty and tranquillity of the hills with what they considered to be riff-raff, but the conditions prevalent for the masses of workers in the early days of the industrial revolution drove working people out to the countryside on their day of rest in their glorious hoards. In the words of the famous song the Manchester Rambler: "I may be a wage slave on Monday but I'm a freeman on Sunday".

In the year 2001 it is inspiring to imagine the picture of Manchester Central station in the 1930's described here, where on any Sunday thousands of walkers would be clamouring to board trains to take them for a day in the hills. We can't go back in time, but those of us who are attempting to cut through the powerful car dependency and lethargy can use this lesson from history to help create a culture in which walking is seen as a valid and healthy form of transport and recreation.

This history ends at the point when the Ramblers' Association officially began. This was when the groundswell had become sufficiently vocal – or should we say sure-footed? – for rambling groups across the country to come together to speak with one voice in the 1930's and 40s. They were led by the great Tom Stephenson and formed the foundations of the movement we are part of today and which has done so much for walkers throughout Britain.

David Hollett has managed to find some wonderful illustrations for this book – they come from many sources and are beautifully reproduced. They tell a story of their own and are a treasure trove.

Nick Barrett

Nick Barrett
Ramblers' Association Chief Executive

INTRODUCTION

Rambling, which is among the most popular of outdoor activities, continues to attract support in ever-increasing numbers. Historically, it owes its establishment to a reaction against mass urbanisation, brought about by the industrial revolution and rural poverty, which drove millions of people into Britain's over-crowded industrial towns and cities. At the weekend, however, they sought escape from the dreary routine of urban existence by returning to the countryside they loved – as ramblers.

Our fascinating trek through rambling and 'Access' history begins in Scotland, in 1850, when two young students had the audacity to challenge the Duke of Atholl's right to deny public access to Glen Tilt. Other chapters on Scotland pay attention to the arrival of tourists in the Highlands; the great confrontation between the American railroad millionaire, W.L. Winans, and Murdo Macrae – over a pet lamb; and James Bryce MP – and his historic campaign for public access to mountains and moorland.

Turning south, the history of the Commons Preservation Society is outlined in some detail. Next to be mentioned are some of our most notable pioneering rambling clubs, for example, Sir Leslie Stephen's Sunday Tramps, established in 1879; the Forest Ramblers' Club, established in 1884; the Yorkshire Rambling Club; the Manchester Rucksack Club, the Sheffield Clarion Ramblers, and many more. Long distance walking and record-breaking marathon walking receive good coverage. A chapter is also dedicated to the Lake District, where Wordsworth and his fellow 'Lakers' did so much to popularise rambling.

Rambling or 'Hiking' reached a high point in the 1930's when thousands left our major cities each weekend to ramble in the countryside. This was also the decade that saw the establishment of the Ramblers' Association, The Youth Hostel Association, and many rambling orientated holiday organisations aimed at attracting young people. The great Mass Trespass' on Kinder Scout took place in 1932, followed by the famous Winnats Pass Access Rallies, all of which notable events are recorded in the text. In short, this is a book that I trust will interest ramblers and all the many thousands of people in Britain who have an interest in the "Great Outdoors."

David Hollett
2002

CHAPTER ONE   THE BATTLE OF GLEN TILT

By the middle years of the 19th century pioneer ramblers, mountaineers and tourists were beginning to head north to the Scottish Highlands. However, in stark contrast to other mountainous countries in Europe, such as Switzerland, where officials did all they could to make such people welcome, the all-powerful Scottish Lairds did just the opposite! To them ramblers, mountaineers and tourists were regarded as unwelcome intruders who had to be kept at bay at all costs.

And the reason for this anti-social behaviour was quite simple. In one historic move the Lairds had driven out the Highland crofters to make way for the then more profitable sheep. But in the second phase of this process these landowners were hard at work once more, but this time getting rid of farmers in order to convert their sheep-walks into now more profitable deer-forests. At the helm in this questionable process were the all-powerful Dukes of Atholl.

Writing about the Highland Clearances in 1883 Alexander Mackenzie quoted an earlier writer, Donald Macleod who, referring to the evictions from land in Perthshire stated: "A Duke of Atholl can, with propriety, claim the origin of the Highland clearances. Whatever merit the family of Sutherland may take to themselves for the fire and the fagot expulsion of the people from the glens of Sutherland, they cannot claim the merit of originality. The present [6th] Duke of Atholl's grandfather cleared Glen Tilt, so far as I can learn, in 1774." (1)

And it was from their feudal stronghold, Blair Castle in Perthshire, that the respective Dukes of Atholl ran their 194,640 acre estate. (2) Now conveniently cleared of crofters, and sheep, but with the addition of an impressive band of keepers and ghillies, this Kingdom-within-a-Kingdom, like a large proportion of the rest

1

of the Scottish Highlands was, by 1847, dedicated to the rearing of deer, for ritual slaughter by the hunting and shooting fraternity. Given this historic scenario there was, of course, no way that men such as Atholl were going to welcome back a new wave of common "intruders" in the form of ramblers or tourists.

To put this into perspective, it should be noted that few creatures, great or small, were welcomed to share the Highlands with these aristocrats. If 'game' animals or birds were not being reared on their vast domains specifically in order to be shot by paying guests, the chances are they were being classified as 'vermin,' unfortunate beings whose continued existence ran counter to the perceived interest of game rearing. Thus, writing in 1930, Hugh S. Gladstone is able to advise us that:

"In olden days vermin was far more plentiful in Great Britain than it is today and the totals killed in a year on some estates sound amazing to us nowadays. The general abstract of vermin killed in the county of Sutherland and on the estates of Langwell and Sandside in the county of Caithness shows that, from 6th July 1819 to 17th August 1826, there were killed 295 old Eagles; 60 young Eagles with eggs; 23 Bitch Foxes in milk; 293 Old Foxes; 230 Cub Foxes; 1,143 Wild Cats, Martens and Polecats; 1,962 Ravens; 1,115 Hawks; 2,647 Carrion Crows and Magpies; 1,799 Rooks and Jackdaws." (3)

The social, economic and environmental consequences of clearing the Scottish Highlands of human beings to make way for deer was, of course, profound, negative and long-lasting. Nevertheless, it was against this medieval, autocratic social background that the first modern-day ramblers tried to claim very modest rights of access to the Highlands of their own country.

One of the first challenges to be mounted against the Highland Laird's policy of excluding the public from their land was made in 1845. This was mounted by an Edinburgh society formed 'for protecting the public against being robbed of its walks by cunning and perseverance.' At first they focussed their attention on 'forbidden' land in the immediate vicinity of Edinburgh. However, they soon found themselves engaged in a protracted legal battle with the 6th Duke of Atholl over a public right of way over land which he owned far to the north of this great city.

The great 200,000 acre estate in question was, or course, the Blair Atholl spread, half of which the noble Duke had converted into a depopulated 'deer-forest'. And running through this isolated, private domain was an old drove road which, not surprisingly, was claimed as an ancient public right of way. Predictably, the Duke of Atholl thought otherwise! All of which was put to the test in 1847 when the Duke tried to prevent Professor Bayley Balfour and a party of botanical students from passing through Glen Tilt. After futile attempts to persuade the Duke to be reasonable had failed, in 1849 the Edinburgh Society decided to take the case to court.

In court the case went against the Duke, declaring that the track through Glen Tilt was indeed, a public right of way. Predictably, the obstinate old Duke petitioned for leave to appeal. But while the case was making its slow, ponderous way through the law courts, Atholl took a hard uncompromising line by instructing his employees to forcibly intercept two Cambridge undergraduates whilst they were attempting to pass through the glen. Two months later, one of the students, writing under the appropriate pseudonym of 'Cantabrigiensis' told the British public about their battle in Glen Tilt. In a long letter to *The Times* the student opened by stating:

"Sir, - It is generally thought that in this land of liberty and civilisation wild men of the woods and savages have long been extinct; the following account of an adventure which lately befell myself and a fellow student on a tour of the Highlands will show the fallacy of the supposition.

On Friday, August 30, [1850] we shouldered our knapsacks and left Castletown of Braemar with the intention of walking to Blair Atholl through Glen Tilt, a distance of 30 miles. We might have gone by another road through Blair Gowrie and Dunkeld, but as this road was upwards of 60 miles in length, and we were informed by all persons of whom we inquired at Braemar that though the Duke of Atholl, in spite of a decision of the Court of Sessions, was still endeavouring to stop all who made use of the Bridleroad or footpath through Glen Tilt, yet he would not dare to use violence if one insisted on a right of passage, we determined to take the shorter road."

Deer stalking in the Highlands – A Sketch in Glen Tilt

Highland Deer-stalking: "By George! Missed again."

The two proceeded down the glen for about twelve miles, until they came to a fast-flowing mountain stream, over which was the remains of a wooden bridge. This, it appears, had been cut down just a few days previously, with the clear intention of stopping pedestrians from proceeding down the glen. Fortunately for the students this deliberate act of destruction had been so imperfectly executed that they both managed to clamber over what was left of the structure without even getting their feet wet.

After walking a further eight miles down the lonely glen they passed the Dukes hunting lodge, at which point their luck ran out. For here they were confronted by a tall kilted ghillie, who jumped in front of them and, with "a bullying and menacing attitude" urged them to go back. 'Cantabrigiensis' responded to this challenge by asking the man his name, which he gave as Alexander

5

Maclarran, who then went on to state that he was acting on the instructions of his employer, the Duke of Atholl who, it would seem, was just below them in the glen.

After a decidedly heated exchange Maclarren then led the two students down the glen to meet the noble Duke in person, whom they eventually found, albeit in a great stare of excitement and determined to oppose their progress, vociferating – "You must go back. Why don't you stop, Sir?" The imperturbable "Cantabrigiensis" responded by taking out his pocket-book. Now prepared to write he said, "What is your name?" No doubt almost purple with rage at the fact that he was actually being challenged to identify himself by a mere mortal, his grace spluttered "I am the Duke of Atholl!" Upon receiving this precious information "Cantabrigiensis" tendered his card, and then stated that they wished to proceed to Blair Atholl. For the rest of this fascinating account of "The Battle of Glen Tilt "Cantabrigiensis's letter to *The Times* is quoted:

"However, he insisted that we must "go back," to which we urged that the Court of Session had decided that there was a right of way through Glen Tilt, and therefore we could not be stopped. He replied angrily, "It is not a public way, it is my private drive; you shan't come down; the deer are coming." Upon this we expressed our willingness to retire behind the lodge till his sport was ended, but he said we had been impertinent, we claimed it as a right, and we should not go down an inch.

"Hereupon I said that in that case I certainly would go down, and if he stopped it would be at his peril, upon which he became impatient, seized my companion by the collar of his coat, and attempted to force him back, refusing to listen to anything we had to say. This unseemly scene took place before the eyes of the Duchess and another lady, for whose presence he had so little regard as to use oaths and other violence such as you would scarcely expect to

6

hear from the lips of a gentleman. Finding his strength was of little avail, he shouted for help to his unwilling grooms, who were evidently enjoying the scene from a distance, and my companion, seeing opposition was useless against four men, allowed ourselves to be led away by a servant.

"The Duke then returned, full of anger, gave me over to a similar escort, and thus we were left to enjoy our reflections at the back of the lodge, while his Grace awaited the descent of his victims from the hills. The old Highlander who had charge of my companion told him the best thing he could do was wait there till nightfall, and then finish the journey to Blair Atholl in the dark. Finding ourselves thus disappointed for the present, we climbed up the steep side of the glen to view the deer as they were driven over the hills to be slaughtered by the noble and gallant butcher below. But, alas! No deer came.

"The Duke had had his sport for that day with us, but he was not yet content. We had been ascending "the brae," and accordingly two ghillies were dispatched after us, who, on coming up, threatened to take us up for poachers, but at length mercifully allowed us to descend the hills and pursue our way back to Castleton, a distance of 20 miles! They told us we would be closely watched, and if we stirred from the path we would be prosecuted for trespassing. On parting, they took good care to tell us that it was not their fault; and I will do them justice to say they did their work very reluctantly.

"Well now, there was nothing to do but to take the old ghillies advice, and wait till dark. The hills on each side were very steep, so that, besides the danger of being taken up for trespass, it would have been no easy matter to find our way to a village distant 10 miles. For four long hours, then, we were forced to walk up and down this bleak vale in order to ward off the chill autumn evening. When it became dark we proceeded on our way, which gave us no

7

little trouble and uncertainty, as the darkness of the night was increased by the black shade of the pine forests. However, by midnight we reached the hotel, and soon recovered from the fatigue of a day which, after all, gave us a good deal of amusement. I should not have ventured to apply for any room in your valuable paper, had I not been frequently urged by my friends to publish my adventure." (4)

Historically, the publication of this well-known event is significant, for it encapsulated the inherent injustice of unrestrained, private rights over open countryside in general, and the social ramifications of this system, which had emerged in an extreme form in the Highlands of Scotland. Unfortunately, in narrow legalistic terms 'Cantabrigiensis' and his companion had misunderstood the outcome of the Court of Sessions Case. This due to the fact that at the time they attempted to pass down the forbidden glen, pending the outcome of the Duke's appeal, the outcome was only that there was a right to bring the case, *not* that the track had been confirmed as a right of way.

Nevertheless, *The Times,* then in radical mode, followed this up two days later by devoting a long leader on the incident, in which the writer more or less repeated the story and then fell into the same trap as the students by assuming that there was, at this point in time, a public right of way through Glen Tilt which, of course, there was not. (5) On a fine point of law the students and *The Times* were technically incorrect, but that misses the point. The essential point being that they were both occupying the moral high ground on a fundamental issue this adventure had spotlighted. The inherent injustice of a social system which allowed one man to control almost 200,000 acres, whilst others, through this same system were being driven, penniless, off this same land, into the slums of Glasgow.

However, other letters, all sympathetic to the students, were soon published in *The Times*, which was then followed by one from

Mr. J. Condie, Land Agent to the Duke. Condie argued, on behalf of his master, that rightly or wrongly, as the law stood, the Duke of Atholl had been acting in accordance with the law. He then went on to argue that the two students had been made particularly aware of these facts. (6) Nevertheless, and quite deservedly, the noble Duke was subsequently lampooned mercilessly in the pages of *Punch*. The following being one of the periodical's best contributions on the issue:

"THE ATHOLL PASSPORT OFFICE"

"An office will shortly be opened in Edinburgh for the purpose of issuing passports to Glen Tilt and other impassable passes of the Atholl estate, it is to be called the Atholl Passport Office. Travellers will be expected to give their names, addresses, and occupations, and motives for travelling, besides finding two sureties for their respectable and good behaviour. Another stipulation also is, that they are to carry neither gun, nor fishing-rod, nor fowling-piece, nor stick, nor sword, nor knife, nor pencil, nor sketching apparatus, as the Duke is determined that nothing, not even a view, shall be carried off his estate – at all events, not till a Court of Law has thrown it open to the public. Every passport will have his Grace's signature and seal, and a price, somewhat less than what is charged by Lord Palmerston for a Foreign Passport, will be demanded for it, so as to keep the country within the walks of the very highest. This measure will have the effect of increasing the Duke's income, even though it should close and make still narrower the respect that is universally felt for the narrowness of his ways, and unenlightened selfishness of his views." (7)

SCENE FROM THE BURLESQUE RECENTLY PERFORMED AT GLEN TILT.
" These are Clan Atholl warriors true,
And, Saxons, I 'm the reg'lar Doo."
Punch 1850

Scene from the Burlesque recently Performed at Glen Tilt. Punch 1850

The satirical lines quoted above may seem harsh, but they are far from so when related to the historical track record of the Dukes of Atholl and Glen Tilt. The aforementioned Cambridge students had merely been prevented from passing through the glen, but it was, as indicated, the 4th Duke who was responsible for ruthlessly clearing Glen Tilt of its inhabitants in 1774, which was, of course, a far more serious matter. All of which may well have been in the minds of satirical writers in 1850!

Atholl's appeal to the House of Lords over this issue was heard on 3rd – 4th June 1852. Unfortunately, for the noble Duke, the decision of the lower court was upheld with costs against the Duke. But due to the complexities of Scottish law this still left undetermined the right of way through Glen Tilt, and merely gave the pursuers, or others the title to prove a right of way. But, apparently, this was not pursued, or considered necessary for, after the Lord's decision, the Duke appeared to lose interest in the case. (8)

The Dukes of Atholl and the Clearances. Prior to the notorious Clearances Glen Tilt, it should be noted, was occupied in the same way as other highland valleys, each family possessing a piece of arable land, while the pasture was held in common. The Highlanders were allowed to fish in the Tilt, and from time immemorial, were accustomed to take cattle, in the summer months, to a higher glen, which is watered by the Tarf. But, unfortunately, the Duke decided to convert Glen Tarf into a deer-forest. Accordingly, he built a high dyke at the head of Glen Tilt, specifically designed to prevent the movement of cattle.

The Duke's deer increased rapidly but when hungry began to destroy the crofter's crops. But instead of taking reasonable steps to keep these animals off the arable land the Duke decided to gratify the healthy appetites of these creatures by adding another thousand acres of the people's land to his private deer forest. Without undue delay Atholl's 'forest' extended, until the people were gradually touted off, and many had to bid farewell to their beautiful glen.

An event then occurred which afforded a pretext to the Duke to get rid of the remaining inhabitants of Glen Tilt at one fell stroke. Highland Chieftains were then raising regiments to serve in the American War, and Atholl felt obligated to do the same. Great efforts were made to enlist the men of Glen Tilt, which included the promise of perpetual possession of their lands, if they would sign up. A few did, but in the main they took the view that they were not going to be dragged by a Chief into a war about which they knew very little. (9) Alexander Mackenzie, the noted 19th Century historian, explains what happened next:

11

"The Duke flew into a rage, and press gangs were sent up the glen to carry off the young men by force. One of these companies seized a crippled tailor, who lived at the foot of Beneygloe, and afraid lest he might carry intelligence of their approach up the glen, they bound him, hand and foot, and left him lying on the cold hillside, where he contracted diseases from which he never recovered. By impressment and violence the regiment was at length raised; and when peace was proclaimed, instead of restoring the soldiers to their friends and homes, the Duke, as if he had been a trafficker in slaves, was only prevented from selling them to the East India Company by the mutiny of the regiment.

"He afterwards pretended great offence at the Glen Tilt people for their obstinacy in refusing to enlist, and it may now be added, to be sold. Their conduct in the affair was given out as the reason why he cleared them out of the glen – an excuse which, in the present day, may increase our admiration of the people, but can never palliate the heartlessness of his conduct. His ireful policy has, however, taken full effect. The romantic Glen Tilt, with its fertile holms and verdant steeps, is little better than a desert. The very deer rarely visit it, and the waste grass is burned like heather, at the beginning of the year, to make room for new verdure. On the spot where I found the grass most luxuriant, I traced the sites of thirty cottages, and have no hesitation in saying, that under skill, the industrious habits, and the agricultural facilities of the present day, the land once occupied by the tenants of Glen Tilt, is capable of maintaining a thousand people and have a large proportion of sheep and cattle for exportation besides. In the meantime it serves no better purpose than the occasional playground of the Duke.

"The glens of Atoll are intersected by smaller valleys, presenting various aspects, from the most fertile carse to the bleakest moorland. But man durst not be seen there. The image of God is forbidden unless it be stamped upon the Duke, his foresters, and gamekeepers, that the deer may not be disturbed." (10)

Needless to say, the Dukes of Atholl were only one family of Highland Chieftains among many who, during the course of the 19th century, continued an already well-established policy of clearing the Highlands and Islands of their 'surplus' population. For example, in 1853 Mr R. Alister had a controversy with the Marquis of Breadalbane about the eviction of his tenantry which, for obvious reasons, he never attempted to answer. The substance of the charge being that between the years of 1834 and 1853 his Lordship had 'removed' 500 families from the Breadalbane estates, all of whom had been thrown out and left without a roof over their heads. (11)

Expulsions on the Duke of Sutherland's estates were particularly severe, added to which was the fact that at one time even marriage was prohibited among the Sutherland peasantry; the penalty for infringing on this rule was prompt expulsion from the estate. In 1807 ninety families were removed from the parishes of Farr and Larg, Sutherland, and in 1813 there were 'removals' in lower Kildonan in the same country. The final clearance of Strathnaver and Upper Kildonan, Sutherland, taking place in 1819. (12)

The arbitrary 'removal' of the Duke of Sutherland, and his fellow Scottish Chieftains, should have been on the agenda, but alas was not. Instead, Sutherland and the rest of them remained in their baronial halls, and continued to amass more money. The Duke of Sutherland's money was, by way of an example, expended for the most astonishing purposes; but not an insignificant proportion of his ill-gotten gains going to entertain carefully selected literary flatterers to vindicate the mal-administration of the Agents to whom he had entrusted the management of his affairs.

The most notable of these was Mrs Harriet Beecher Stowe, the celebrated campaigner against slavery in the United States who, in 1856, on her second visit to Britain, stayed at Inverary and Dunrobin to gather 'Notes on the Clearances' which she published in *Sunny Memories*. When referring to the so-called "Sutherland Improvements," [Clearances] Mrs Stowe dutifully wrote, and with a truly amazing disregard for the real facts:

"To my view it is almost a sublime instance of the benevolent employment of superior wealth and power in shortening the struggles of civilisation, and elevating in a few years a whole community to a point of education and material prosperity, which, unassisted, they might never have obtained." (13) Needless to say, those recently evicted from the Sutherland estates, left homeless and destitute, and without any form of 'material prosperity' whatsoever, tended to view these developments in a somewhat different light.

Unfortunately, Beecher Stowe was only one among many well-known writers to be wined and dined by a Scottish Laird in what were, very clearly, staged managed 'Public Relations' exercises. By way of a further example was our old 'Lakeland' friend, Harriet Martineau who, after being wined and dined by Lord Murray at his seat in Argyleshire, subsequently repaid her hospitality debt by writing:

"While at Strathur, Lord Murray's seat in Argyllshire, we found ourselves treated with singular hospitality. Lord Murray placed the little Loch Fine steamer at our disposal. He and Lady Murray insisted on receiving our entire party; and every facility was afforded for all of us seeing everything. Every Highland production, in the form of fish, flesh and fowl, was carefully collected: salmon and loch herrings, grouse pies, and red deer soup and so forth." (14)

By way of contrast, however, whilst Harriet Martineau was feasting herself on grouse pies and red deer soup, many of the Highland people, in the middle-years of the 19th Century, were trying to exist upon a diet of boiled grass and nettles. And conditions were even worse in the back streets of the Scottish towns and cities, where many of the evicted Highlanders had been forced to take up residence.

Within a circle of twelve miles of Glasgow there were, in 1861, no less than ten thousand "paupers" receiving on average not more that one shilling and sixpence a week. And it was in these areas that the children of the evictions, the child serfs in the West of Scotland bleach-fields, were being worked from eleven to eighteen hours daily in stoves heated from eighty to a hundred degrees. At Pollockshaws children were occasionally worked two and three days and nights consecutively. The Establishment, however, was not entirely heartless, for the Whig Act of 1851 *did* regulate magisterial punishment of young children to a maximum of just thirty lashes! Not surprisingly, 50% of young children died under these conditions before they were five years old.

In the first forty years of the 19th Century it is estimated some three hundred and forty thousand strangers were huddled together on the banks of the Clyde, where they suffered periodic decimation by Typhus. In 1840 children of eleven years worked from 5 a.m. to 5 p.m. A girl, Ellison Jack, of Loanhead Colliery, began at the age of eight to work from 2 a.m. till 1 p.m. or 2 p.m. And about these pits, where such children toiled it was written:

"The pit bottoms are like common sewers, slush and water, with an inclination of one in three, and along these common sewers, the women, half-naked, crawled on hands and knees, harnessed like horses to their bogies of coals. Little boys, aged four or five, sit all day in the darkness at the trap-doors, cold and shivering, begging for a candle-end for light..." (15)

The glens had indeed been cleared, but at an awful cost in human suffering. But during the second part of the 19th Century the Highlands were being re-occupied at an ever-increasing pace by human beings. This influx was, alas, only a seasonal one that was, inevitably, led by those for whom the glens had been cleared – the affluent, upper-class shooters of deer and grouse. However, middle-class ramblers, tourists and climbers soon followed. Then, towards the close of the 19th Century working-class ramblers, firstly from Edinburgh and Glasgow, were to follow in the footsteps of the more affluent. The long trek north to gaze in awe at the beauty of the now lonely and de-populated Scottish Highlands had begun.

Tourists on board a Highland steamer, 1871

CHAPTER TWO   HEADING FOR THE HIGHLANDS

The long trek north to the Scottish Highlands really got under way in the second part of the 19th century. The hunting and shooting fraternity were, of course, in the advance guard of this seasonal migration. But they were increasingly accompanied on the long journey to the north by middle class tourists, mountaineers, ramblers, and others. Then, towards the close of the 19th century, working class ramblers, from Glasgow and Edinburgh, began to head in the same direction.

The only question was how to get there! Many who could afford it chose to go by the 'Royal Route' – that is on board the scheduled mail-steamer *Iona,* which ran a regular service from Glasgow to the Highlands, via places such as Ballachulish, and Auchnasheen. The Highlands were clearly *the* fashionable place to go, as the following lines, advocating a trip north, published in *The Illustrated London News* in the summer of 1871indicate:

"In the Highlands: Although the Session is not quite over, the Season is, and London is emptying fast. Next week not a single soul will be found in it, except the two or three millions of nobodies, hewers of wood and drawers of water, to whom holiday – except a flying visit, at long intervals, to Gravesend or Southend – is an empty sound. Yet these brief and far-between outings leave some trails of glory on their lives. What is there in London worth living for, with the opera-houses closed and Rotten-row a desert?"

On board the *Iona,* our fashionable writer took a glance at his fellow passengers, and concluded they were a very motley crowd. Near the helmsman he noted someone, he concluded by his talk, to be an owner or renter of a snug shooting box deep in the Highlands, attended by his fair daughter! He also spotted salmon-fishers; youths fresh from 'Cockneydom,' who had tried to disguise themselves in Scottish garb; the inevitable 'Yankee' tourist, artists; and, here and there alas:

"Scattered among the lively, loving family groups, may be found, it is to be feared, a cad or two; but never mind them, they must be unimprovable indeed if they do not drop some of their self-conceit amid the scenes they will presently visit, and mellow into something higher and nobler than they had ever conceived." (1)

Not to be outdone, two years later, in the autumn of 1873, *The Graphic,* rival periodical to the *Illustrated London News,* sent their talented artist up north to sample the delights of a trip from Glasgow to Oban on D. Hutcheson and Co.'s ship the *Iona.* " 'See Naples and Die,' " says our artist, "is a Neapolitan proverb which must have been made before the *Iona* was built – anyway before you die try a trip from Glasgow to Oban, and you'll conclude to take a fresh lease on life." This artist and writer also noted the ship was carrying an amazing variety of people, which ranged from, working men having a day trip, to peers heading north for the deer-stalking. It is also interesting to note, that even in 1873, the ship was also carrying many American, Japanese, French and German tourists! (2)

A tour in Scotland: On board the Iona, Glasgow to Oban, 1873

19

Inevitably, the ascent of Ben Nevis became a prime objective of the early tourists and walkers in the second part of the 19th century. The views from the summit, when once gained, tourists were assured, are "sublimely vast" extending over large sections of Argyllshire and Inverness-shire. In 1881 ramblers who were 'athletic' as well as lovers of the 'romantic and picturesque' were assured that they could walk all the way to the top, to see if they liked it, *or* take a more civilised option. Namely, to ride half way up on ponies to the 'tarn' which is called Loch an-t' Suidhe. One party who bravely opted for the 'Athletic Option' in 1881 was an army Major and his genteel entourage. Unfortunately, they were intercepted at the half-way point by a reporter and artist from *The Illustrated London News*. He wrote: "suppose ourselves to be up there just now, and whom do we meet" and he continued:

"Our friend the Major, ever prompt and bland, attired in a complete suit of tartan checkered dittos, cap and gaiters included. He has grown a trifle more plump in the body, and more puffy in the face, than when we last saw him three years ago, upon his retirement from the active list. But the briskness of his gestures is still unabated, and it is with a more knowing look than ever, that he sticks the glass in his eye; not for an elegant nose like his were spectacles invented!

"The young lady besides him is Miss Florence his niece, and her brother Walter, a Cantab undergraduate, is one of those behind. Their father being in India, and the Major nothing better to do in August, he has arranged with their maternal parent, who is an invalid, to superintend this Highland tour. Walter's schoolfellow at Rugby three years ago, Charley Bond, with his sister, Miss Katie, and early friend of Miss Florence, have been permitted to join the party, coming on together from Carlisle to Glasgow, and thence by steam-boat to Oban, with further wanderings in the West Highlands during the past week. And here they are, on a fine bright sunny morning, half-way up the height of Ben Nevis! They are escorted by a trusty local guide, Peter Cameron, of Lochiel, who carries a basket of provisions on his back as he walks after the party." (3)

The 'hotel' and observatory on the summit of Ben Nevis, 1885.

The Major and his genteel entourage climbing Ben Nevis, 1881

Meanwhile, whilst the English and Scottish upper and middle-classes made their way north to enjoy the delights of the Scottish Highlands, leading lights of the Scottish, urban working classes were also just beginning to set their sights on this delightful part of their own country. All of which brings us to the moving story of Hugh Macdonald, pioneer Scottish rambler.

To put this remarkable story into historical perspective it should be noted that, among other things, the Scottish Census Returns for 1861 showed that one-third of the population of Scotland lived in single-roomed 'houses' or, to be more precise, 'hovels.' And seven thousand nine hundred and sixty four of these had no windows. In Port Glasgow a stable had been converted into a dwelling-house, and during the whole summer that stable contained eighty-three persons, as well as the horse! (4)

Given such conditions, in post-clearance and early industrial Scotland, it seems unlikely, almost to the point of being inconceivable, that a working-man could have found the time and energy to develop an interest in rambling. Nevertheless, and against all odds, Hugh Macdonald emerged to play this pioneering role in the history of British Rambling.

Hugh Macdonald did not feature in the Census of 1861 for he died in 1860, at the early age of forty-three. Born at Rumford Street, Bridgetown, Glasgow, on 4th of April, 1817, this remarkable man was the eldest of eleven children, born to Malcolm Macdonald and his wife, Margaret M'lean. Little is known about the background of this working-class couple except that they came from the West Highlands and, therefore could, quite possibly, have been victims of the clearances, or economic refugees which, in practice, often amounted to almost the same thing. Typically, young Hugh Macdonald's formal school education ceased when the reached to age of nine, though at a later date he attended what were known as 'continuation classes'.

Hugh Macdonald's great friend, Alexander Smith, however, has told us, in his *Summer in Skye,* but for reasons that are not explained, that as a youth Macdonald lived for a time on the beautiful Isle of Mull, all of which is confirmed by Macdonald. In the *Morning Journal* of 8th September 1859 there was published the third instalment of Macdonald's *A Trip to the Western Highlands,* in the course of which he confirms that as a boy he spent time on Mull.

On returning to his native city, however, the young Macdonald was apprenticed to the block-printing business with Henry Monteith & Company, one of the most prosperous firms of its kind. It was a respected craft, well-paid as wages went then, but this has to be seen in the context of the industry as a whole. Attached to every calico printing factory there was a bleachfield, which was the name popularly given to the whole of such establishments, and in which young children were worked brutally for a pittance, and for up to eighteen hours a day.

Yet even as a lad Macdonald was a keen rambler, and he later became a noted poet and writer. With Macdonald (as with many others) his literary life began in verses, many of his early efforts were, in fact, published in the columns of the radical paper *Chartist Circular.* For a time, it is very interesting to note, the six points of the People's Charter, and the Chartist campaigners, were seen by Macdonald, and thousands of his fellow toilers, as the movement that was destined to sweep away the old society and herald the arrival of the millennium. (5)

In the year of 1848 Macdonald's fortunes were at a low point, for in that year he opened a small provision shop in Bridgetown, and due to being too generous in the granting of credit lost every penny he had. But Macdonald bounced back. He paid all his debts and then, just a few years later, his lucky-break came when he was appointed sub-editor of the *Glasgow Citizen.*

One of the first fruits of his appointment was the appearance, in the columns of the *Citizen,* a long series of *Rambles Round Glasgow*, by Hugh Macdonald, but under the signature of 'Caleb.' Apart from an 'introductory' item published on 7th June, 1851, the first of the actual series appeared on 14th June, 1851, which was entitled *The Banks of the Clyde- Carmyle and Kenmuir.* In all there were twenty-three articles, the last of which was *Paisley and Environs,* which appeared on 22nd October, 1853. The articles aroused much interest, to the extent that they were published in book form in 1854; a second was issued in 1856 and from then on, throughout Glasgow and the West of Scotland, *Macdonald's Rambles* has been a household word.

His *Rambles* are rich in antiquarian lore and they are equally rich in literary interests, Macdonald, a poor man from a poor family, who left school at the age of nine, nevertheless displayed a mastery of English that is as excellent as it is rare. But perhaps the most charming feature of the *Rambles* is not their wealth of lore, nor their poetic glamour, but the revelation throughout his writings of a most loveable and genial personality.   Also apparent throughout is Macdonald's vivid sense of comradeship. And, as his biographer, the Rev. Morrison very aptly put it – "It is a great thing when rambling to have congenial company" which was clear from all he wrote, this was something that Macdonald very much appreciated. (6)

For a period of about six years Macdonald maintained his connection with the *Citizen,* but he left it in 1855 to take up a more responsible post, that of Editor of the *Glasgow Times.* Hugh Macdonald was married twice. His first wife was Agnes Macdonald whom he married in 1842. Tragically, she died the following year. Then, in accordance with the wishes of Agnes, in 1846 he married Agnes Macdonald's closest friend, Alison Couper (1819-1887). The couple had five children.

On his death a fund was started on behalf of his widow and children, and it shows the affection in which Macdonald was held that in a very short time it amounted to £900. (7) Without a doubt, Hugh Macdonald was one of the pioneers of the rambling movement in Scotland. He had set things in motion by inspiring others. Consequently, just over three decades after he died in 1860, the West of Scotland witnessed the launching of a Ramblers' Alliance.

It was, in fact, in late December, 1892 that the Glasgow press advised the public that a conference had just taken place under the auspices of a recently formed organisation calling itself 'The Scottish Ramblers Alliance' on the advantages of rambling as a means of recreation and education. Clearly organised by the church, and a group of middle-class intellectuals, the meeting was held in the Christian Institute, Glasgow. Apparently, the meeting had been well attended. A Professor Drumond presided, and among those on the platform was the Rev. Professor Lindsay, together with five other ministers of the church, one or two other notables, and a Mr R. Henderson Smith, Y.M.C.A. 'Travelling Secretary.' Opening the proceedings the chairman began by explaining that they were there to "frame and consolidate another scheme to patch up the much patched-up world." But, the audience were assured, they did not propose to make any violent departures! He continued:

"One of the first things required was the capacity to walk. They wanted to make their summer rambles on a Saturday afternoons not only recreational but educative and to some extent social, and for that purpose there were already at least ten clubs, he understood, within a few miles of Glasgow. It had occurred to the genius of Mr White – (Applause) – that the work of these clubs could be more efficiently performed and their influence extended if they formed themselves into an alliance. That had now been done and they were met to discuss their prospects and expound their objects to the world." (8)

All of which was not quite as spontaneous as it appears, for the rambling clubs represented at this meeting were just those that had already been established by the United Presbyterian Churches and the Y.M.C.A. (9) And in heading this movement up by forming themselves into a formal "Alliance" the leaders of these religious organisations were, among other things, able to ensure that their working-class members continued to confine their walking to a Saturday afternoon!

Another most desirable feature of these clubs was that they encouraged all members to make walks "effective, in a scientific direction," and in this connection the chairman urged participants to study botany, biology and geology, and make a modest contribution to these sciences! No doubt inadvertently, there was also an added bonus here, insofar that whilst thus engaged they would not have the time or energy to follow those who were intent on making more radical, socialistic efforts to alter this "much patched-up world."

Nevertheless, for its day, this religious rambling alliance was, in its own way moderately radical, and notably for the way that it acknowledged the existence of women! For, as the chairman put it in his concluding remarks, "he was glad that the Alliance had added lady members, so that they might be quite sure that the evolution of the social side would be carried to its utmost capacity." (10) Four years later, in 1896, another group of rambling clubs, came together to form an 'Alliance' this one being organised by the Men's Meeting and Literary Association of the Edinburgh West End Mission who, like the Glasgow Alliance, also confined their walking to a few hours on a Saturday afternoon. In the meantime, however, in 1887, James Bryce, with others, had established the celebrated 'Cairngorm Club' – the pioneering Scottish mountain climbing and rambling group, which made no attempt whatsoever to confine their programme to a few hours on a Saturday afternoon!

CHAPTER THREE   WINANS VERSUS MURDO MACRAE

The celebrated case of W. L. Winans, an American Railroad Millionaire, versus Murdo Macrae, a poor Highland cottar and shoe maker, is popularly known as the 'Pet Lamb Case'. It can only be properly understood in the context of matters already outlined, namely, the clearing of the glens, specifically for the creation of vast, de-populated 'Deer Forests'. Of particular significance is the fact that the action was raised in the Dingwall Sheriff Court in 1883. The year of 'Her Majesty's Commission of Inquiry into the conditions of the Crofters and Cottars in the Highlands and Islands of Scotland,' which was commonly known as "The Napier Commission," after Francis, Baron Napier, who headed this revealing investigation.

The case itself, which was based on Murdo Macrae's pet lamb inadvertently straying on to Winans' vast, sacred 'Deer Forest,' succinctly spotlighted the whole question of land ownership, tenants rights, and public access to land. And not only in Scotland – throughout Britain! Land reform, and access to land was then well and truly to the fore on the political agenda. Consequently, the case occupies a unique niche in political history generally, but a particularly special place in the history of the British rambling movement. Specifically, because James Bryce MP, campaigner for open access to mountain and moorland clearly had this case in mind when he presented his famous 'Access to Mountains (Scotland) Bill' to Parliament, just twelve months later. (1)

Although the Commissioners sought to confine their report to the effect of deer forests upon crofters and cottars only, so as to keep within the limits of their narrow remit, this was, in practice, found to be impossible. As they were soon bound to concede, the social and economic aspects of the issue were presented at every turn.

INTERIOR OF A CROFTER'S HUT.

Interior of a crofter's hut, Island of Lewis, 1888

The principal objection advanced against deer forests by the crofters were (a) That they had been created, to a great extent, by the eviction and removal of the inhabitants, and have been the cause of depopulation;   (b) That land cleared for deer, should be made available for crofters;   (c) That in some places, where deer forests, contiguous to arable land in the occupation of crofters, damage was done by deer;   (e) That deer deteriorate the pasture;   (f) and that the temporary employment of gillies and others in connection with the Deer Forests has a demoralising effect (2)

Evidence presented by the Lairds opposing these points included the argument that in deer forests, besides the regular foresters or keepers, there were a considerable number of gillies employed for two months every year. And, many of these let their

29

ponies for hire, and earned from six shillings to seven shillings and six pence per day! (Needless to say, no mention was made about their lack of income for the remaining ten months of the year.) About the issues, the Commissioners wrote:

"We next have to inquire whether deer forests are of substantial benefit to the various classes which compose the community in the Highlands. There can be no doubt that in the case of the landowners that is so. If it were otherwise they would clearly not let their land for the purpose. The advantage is particularly felt at the present moment, when sheep farms are difficult to let. The causes which have led to this difficulty may be shortly stated as follows: The high price of sheep and the low price of wool, means that a farmer has to find a larger capital than formerly." (3)

It was then argued that a very large expenditure had been effected, both by owners and lessees of deer forests, on the creation of roads, and tracks etc., which, it was inferred, was of great benefit to the entire community. The crofters countered this by arguing that the creation of the deer forests was not only depriving them of their homes and livelihood, but also depriving the nation as a whole of the beef, mutton and wool that could have been produced in the glens, had they not been set aside, more or less exclusively, for the rearing and shooting of deer.

Such arguments were not difficult to counter, when one took into account that Great Britain then had at her disposal a vast, food producing empire. Nevertheless, the Commissioners chose to respond to this point by stating that:

"The soil of a whole country, even of a whole region here, might be laid to waste, and the deficit would be promptly covered by the dispatch of grain from Manitoba, and meat from Texas or Australia." Nevertheless, and to their credit, they promptly qualified this by stating: "Yet who would admit that Scotland should be made a wilderness, even if the inhabitants were provided with better lands and more lucrative occupations elsewhere? No one could contemplate the conversion of the whole extent of good pasture, and possibly arable land, at a moderate elevation in the Highlands into forests without alarm." (4)

Unfortunately, during the remaining years of the 19th century many Lairds and wealthy lessees of deer forests did, quite easily, contemplate such a situation which, in opposition to the findings and recommendations of the Napier Commission, continued to convert vast tracks of Scotland into private deer forests, irrespective of the social unrest they were causing. And foremost among these shooting lessees was the American railroad millionaire, William Louis Winans from Baltimore who, in a remarkable attempt to emulate William the Conqueror, was personally responsible for clearing four hundred square miles of Scotland of both tenants and tourists. His vast, albeit leased domain, being one in which neither resident crofter, or visiting mountaineers, ramblers or tourists were welcome, for this land was set aside for his own personal amusement.

The drama which was about to unfold, in which Winans and Macrae were to be the star players, took place on the 12,220 acre Kintail estate, (5) which Winans had leased from J.T. Mackenzie, to form part of his deer-stalking theme-park. Yet another clearance was at the centre of this particular dispute, but this is not meant to imply that 'clearances' were anything new to this particular estate, for the compilers of the *New Statistical Account,* written in 1836, which was quoted by the 'Napier Commission' in 1884, noted that on this estate:-

"A great change has certainly taken place in the worldly circumstances of the people since the last statistical account of the parish was drawn up. Then almost every respectable householder paid rent to the Laird, and all were in easy, happy, and comparatively affluent circumstances. The contrary is now too often the case. Rents were raised, the people became poor, they were either deprived of or voluntarily gave up their possessions. And many of them who were in good circumstances, with from six to ten and even sixteen milch cows, with horses, goats, sheep &c., have since died in poverty, or now live in penury; and yet, strange as it may seem, in manners and dress there is the greatest improvement." (6)

The Winans family of Baltimore, Maryland. The famous Winans family of Baltimore were direct descendants of Jan Wynans who came to America from the Netherlands about 1662. Ross Winans (1796-1877) first became involved with the Baltimore and Ohio Railroad in 1828, becoming the Chief Engineer of this concern just one year later. In 1848, he produced the powerful 'Camelback' locomotive, noted for power on steep grades. In 1843 he was invited to go to Russia to furnish rolling stock for the railroad between Moscow and St. Petersburgh. He declined, but sent his sons, Thomas De Kay Winans and William in his stead, commissioning them with the delivery of a locomotive built for this line.

Thomas Winans, against the competition of all foreign bidders, secured the contract to equip the Russian railroad in five years with locomotives and other rolling stock. One contract led to another, so that orders approximating nearly $2,000,000, which included all the cast iron for the first permanent bridge over the Neva at St. Petersburgh, were added to the original award.

In Russia, on 23rd August, 1847, Thomas Winans married Celeste Revillon, a Russian of French and Italian descent. They had four children. In 1851 Thomas returned to America leaving William to fulfil the remaining contracts, which were completed in 1862. In 1866 the family firm was recalled to Russia under a new contract of eight years duration, but in 1868 the government took over their interests by paying them a very large sum. (7)

The now exceptionally rich Thomas De Kay Winans thenceforth resided in Baltimore, Maryland, at his town house 'Alexandroffsky,' or at his country residence near Baltimore, which he named 'Crimea.' (8) Unfortunately for Scotland, however, his now equally rich brother, William Louis Winans subsequently settled in Great Britain, where he lived until he died in 1897. (9) But this, alas, was not before he had spent many happy years persecuting ill-fated deer, and equally ill-fated Highlanders, who were all unfortunate enough to live on the vast Highland estates over which Winans gained almost total control.

At the peak of his deer-stalking career Winans had a residence in London and two palatial homes in Scotland, one being at Phoineas in Kiltarlity, the other being at Braulen in Strathfarrar, both of which he held on lease from local owners. He was also the lessee of the deer forest at Braulen, owned by Lord Lovat, and the forests of Fasnakle, Afric and Benula from the Chisholm. And last, but far from least, he held on lease from James Thomas Mackenzie of Kintail and Glenmuick the Kintail deer forest. And it was the latter, as already noted, which was the one at the centre of this dispute. In total, Winans managed to gain effective control over a vast territory, stretching almost from coast to coast and, according to his own estimates, it all added up to about 200,000 acres, or 350 square miles!

The Landlord of Kintail, James Thompson Mackenzie, purchased the estate in 1868 and removed the tenants at the expiry of their leases to convert their farms into deer forests. All of which indicates that a new, 'refined' process of clearing the glens was already well in hand, long before Winans set foot in the forest. For it was, in fact, only at Whitsunday, 1882 that Mackenzie let the whole of the great Kintail estate to Winans, with its fishing and shooting rights – and surviving tenants. (10)   Unfortunately, Winans, the lessee, was to be even more ruthless than the owners of the lands he held on lease, insofar as clearing out 'surplus' tenants was concerned.

Giving evidence about this at the Commission of Inquiry was Colin Chisholm, a retired Customs-House Officer of Inverness. Born and brought up at Lietrie, Glancannich, county of Inverness, he stated that according to the press "Mr. Winans, by the simple process of outbidding all competitors, had turned nearly 250,000 acres in the counties of Ross and Inverness into a deer forest. Chisholm then went on to say that prior to the conversion of this area he had seen superior cattle and sheep reared in this great glen, together with excellent crops of oats, potatoes and turnips. But all that he could now see from the road through the glen was half-tame deer browsing at ease among the crumbling walls, and empty but substantial homes, still standing at intervals, with their windows bolted and their doors locked up.

Chisholm then added that even the cattle drovers had been adversely affected by the arrival of Winans. All the cattle and sheep landed on the Lochalsh side of Kyleakin, and intended for the Muir of Ord and other eastern markets, were driven through Lochalsh and Glenelchag till they reached Duilig, in total a distance of about seventeen miles from Balamacara. Here, unfortunately, the drovers encountered a difficulty, namely, whether to drive the sheep or cattle along the old easy road through Coireach, or whether to take them over the rough hills of Carn-na-breabaig. Chisholm then went on to explain more precisely the nature of the 'difficulty.'

The Prince of Wales shooting in the Highlands in 1880

"As Coireach is converted into what Mr Winans calls a sanctuary for deer, I believe that gentleman would rather see a drove pass through his drawing room than by the above route. The drover wishing to avoid the displeasure of Mr. Winans, turns his drove to the steep Bealach-of-Sgairlaire, and drives his stock through the rough high hills of Carn-na-breabaig, Leacinn-na-guaille and Glassletter. Then through Glencannich, in which glen there are stations fenced with iron wire where droves of cattle or sheep are secured at night to prevent them from trespassing on forest ground. There being no accommodation provided in the deer forest for the men in charge of the droves nor for any other men... From Balamacara Hotel, Lochalsh, to Cannich Bridge Inn, Strathglass, a distance of about 40 miles, I believe neither drover nor traveller can buy one pennyworth of meat or drink." (11)

Later in the hearing Chisholm was asked if he knew anything about the Kintail Estate, then held on lease by Winans. He stated that he had been there on many occasions in his boyhood, and had been back there just two years previously. On this occasion, he added, he was saddened to find that that part of the county – Strathglas, Glenshiel, and so on, were practically one vast deer forest, in which, if you passed off a bridle path, one was in danger of being 'collared.'

Chisholm then went on to tell the hearing that Winans actually employed so many well-paid "Watchers" that one could not go within half or a quarter of a mile of his domain without being confronted by a keeper or watcher. He then claimed that he was even cautioned about going off the road a little distance to a spring to take a drink of cold water! But the most astonishing case of all, given in evidence by Chisholm, was that of an artist he knew who had been accused by Winans of stealing his midges!

"I knew of an instance by a Glasgow artist and naturalist who took lodgings for a few days at Cannich Inn, and by instinct or some other way he went up and took himself out of sight of this public house, and when the man found himself in sight of a beautiful clump of heather he started a number of little flies, small and large, and his misfortune was that this great sportsman [Winans] saw him from the hill. He sent a man down, brought him before him, and I don't know what he threatened to do for robbing him of his midges.

"The result was that when the Glasgow man got himself to the Queens' highway there was a battle of very high words, and the people present thought it would end in heavy blows, and they were prepared to save lives on either side. The flies were dead; but the Glasgow man took every one of them to the road, and then he told Mr. Winans that he was not pleased with him at all. And, it was very nearly coming to the greatest battle we ever had in Strathglas for an age – "The Battle of the Midges." (12)

Considering that Winans – newly-established 'Monarch-of the-Glens' – was prepared to take an over-possessive stand over 'his' midges, we should not be the least bit surprised by the fact he was subsequently prepared to take a zero-tolerance line aimed directly at Murdo Macrae's delinquent pet lamb. But who was Murdo Macrae, the poor Highlander, who was brave enough to openly confront Winans, the gun-slinging, autocratic American millionaire?

As well as being a 'Cottar,' Murdo, or Murdock Macrae, was a shoemaker who had built his house at Carn Gorm some twenty years before, this probably being about 1863. He was known, and is still remembered locally, down to the present day, by his Gaelic name of Murchadh Ruadh. Born in 1825, he was, of course, fifty-eight years old when he gave evidence before the Napier Commission, where he was one of the star witnesses. It was through the evidence of courageous men, such as Murdo Macrae, that the world heard for the first time the voice of the downtrodden

Highland poor. And Murdo Macrae was a good spokesman. When giving his evidence before Sir Kenneth Mackenzie, Chairman of the Commission, he opened by stating that since Winans gained control of the land at Kintail only four acres had been left at the disposal of nineteen households for the growing of potatoes or other crops. He continued:

"All the lands of Morvich and Inchewe have been let to Mr. Winans, who has endeavoured to compel the proprietors to turn all the cottars out of house and home. The history of the "Kintail Crofters" case is so well known that it need not be further referred to. The proprietor does not seem to have made any stipulation in his agreement with Mr Winans for their being to remain on the ground, which he might easily have done. While the cottars can scarcely get a bit of land at Morvich, which is admirably adapted for the use of crofters, and which might have been given to them without any damage to the deer forest." (13)

It was, of course, quite clear to Murdo Macrae, and his fellow cottars, that Winans wanted to get rid of them. For when Winans took occupation, under the lease, he engaged his own staff who were under strict instructions to ruthlessly enforce his prohibition against grazing or keeping stock on his forest and, in particular, the former farm at Morvich. To further exacerbate matters, according to Winans' anti-social ruling, the deer forest extended to the high-water mark of Loch Duich, on the shore of which stretch of water the cottars' houses were placed. Which meant, according to the savage terms of the Mackenzie-Winans agreement that as soon as the occupants stepped outside their homes they were trespassing in Winans' forest!

Directly under Mackenzie things had been bad enough, for prior to the arrival of Winans he had already made a ruling which banned the cottars from grazing cattle and sheep on the estate land. But, as a 'generous' concession he had allowed them to graze cattle and sheep on the roadside verges, but even this was to be prohibited under the Winans regime. It was when under such unethical pressure to quit their homes that the famous incident centred on Murdo Macrae's pet lamb occurred.

The saga actually began on a day in May 1882, when Murdo was out cutting peat and, by chance, happened to find a weakly, stray lamb. Taking pity on the small creature, Murdo took it home, where it was nursed back to health, and soon became a family pet. Naturally, on occasion, the lamb left the house and, apparently, being unaware of the terms of the Mackenzie-Winans lease, did what came naturally, ate grass near its owner's cottage, and thus, quite shamelessly, trespassed on Winans' sacred deer forest!

As might be expected, the criminal tendencies of the pet lamb were soon brought to the attention of Winans, who promptly instructed his stalker, William Ross, to order Murdo to impound the lamb. Murdo refused to comply with the demand. Winans responded and on 1st August, 1883, Duncan MacDonald, a sheriff officer from Dingwall, arrived at Carn Gorm and advised the courageous cottar that if he did not get rid of the lamb he would be sent to prison. He then served a summons of interdict on Macrae, and the following day the lamb was taken to Dingwall, where it was sold. Proof commenced at Dingwall on 4th March 1884 under Sheriff Substitute Hill. Quite amazingly, however, both Mackenzie and Winans were allowed to give their evidence before a Commissioner in London. Which arrangement, no doubt, was specifically set up to save them from having to run the gauntlet of a crowd of Murdo Macrae supporters, which was likely, should they have attended a hearing in Scotland.

Mackenzie was somewhat vague in his evidence and admitted to the fact that since purchasing the Kintail estate he had only been to the place on four occasions, and consequently he did not know of Murdo Macrae or where he lived. To his credit, however, Mackenzie then went on to rapidly distance himself from Winans by stating that he considered Winans argument that one small lamb could damage the forest to be absurd. Mackenzie then claimed that when he first heard of the intended action he offered to cancel the lease. Mackenzie then maintained that the cottars did have rights to keep stock through usage and custom. Ostensibly, a line that lent welcome support to the cottars, but one that was doubtful under Scotland's medieval legal system. (14)

Mackenzie's apparently noble stance also does tend to ignore the fact that he had made no reference to such traditional rights of 'usage and custom' when he had been engaged in clearing the same estate of surplus tenants. And all in order to create the forest he subsequently leased to the American! It also implies that he was not totally aware of the ruthless terms of the lease that he was a party to. On which point, the exchange between the commissioners and Chisholm, as to who was more blameworthy, is revealing:

" Well now, I have heard Mr Winans spoken of with some severity on account of his avidity in adding land for the purpose of a forest. But in your opinion, if it is to be blameworthy at all to have forests, to make them and to hold them, is the person who takes the land or the person who holds it more to blame? Is Mr Winans, the lessee, in your opinion, more to blame, or are the proprietors more to blame who accept his terms? The proprietors are in the first place to blame, and he is to blame for straining the law to have every soul and every beast cleared off the land for him; so that the blame must be divided in his case between himself and the landlord." (15)

Winans in his evidence made much of the supposed disturbance that sheep could cause in a deer forest. He claimed that the keeping of one pet lamb could lead to the keeping of many, until there was a very considerable sheep stock being kept in the forest, and on ground that was required for wintering deer. He was then

40

cross-examined as to whether pet lambs were really any more disturbance to the deer than cottars such as Macrae. Without stopping to consider the implications of this line of questioning Winans fell onto the trap. His mask slipped and, no doubt inadvertently, he revealed his true purpose, and general attitude to the poor Highlanders.

He replied: *"What I desire is to get rid of the cottages and their inhabitants: I shan't leave a stone unturned until I get rid of them."*

The Sheriff Substitute issued his judgement on 16th January 1885, finding in favour of Murdo Macrae, and awarding expenses against Winans, who then, quite predictably, proceeded to appeal. At this hearing, conducted by Sheriff Principal Mackintosh, this judgement was reversed, for he found in favour of Winans, with expenses, whereupon Macrae appealed to the Court of Sessions, who reinstated the earlier judgement. The humble cottar, Murdo Macrae, had taken on the multi-millionaire Winans, and defeated him. The still outstanding mystery being how this poor Highlander found the money to defend the action and the two appeals?

The most accepted theory was that it was a wealthy Scot, who had made his money in some foreign land, who had then acted as an anonymous backer. For it was known that some people in this category had helped the Land League and the victims of the 'Land War' which raged throughout the U.K. in the 1880's and 1890's. And, notably, a local variant of this movement was very active, in the Highlands and Islands of Scotland during this period. Re-division of land being the radical, and for the landowners, highly disturbing demand! Public opinion was, however, now running strongly against Winans, all of which was revealed by a small item in *The Times,* which was published four months after he had lost out in the Court of Sessions. It said:

"The action of Mr Winans in closing up a road at Guisachen has caused great indignation in the north. It was reported by a Beauly correspondent that on Saturday evening, while Mr Winans was proceeding through the village of Tomich, near Guisachen, stones were thrown at him. It added that he immediately offered a reward of £500 for the capture or discovery of the guilty persons." (16)

Possibly, in order to show the Scottish landowner, Mackenzie, in a better light, I.R. Mackay of the Gaelic Society of Inverness, advanced the theory that it was Mackenzie, owner of the Kintail estate, who was one of those who helped to pay Macraes court costs. This, however, seems unlikely, for Mackay also states that in 1891 a break occurred in the Mackenzie-Winans lease, and Winans, perhaps wisely, took the opportunity to get out.

Understandably, the cottars then took the opportunity provided by the lease break to get in! They promptly applied to Mackenzie to be allowed a piece of the Morvich low ground but without success! All of which hardly indicates that his attitude to cottars and crofters was so outstandingly positive that he would have backed Macrae with cash in his legal battle against Winans. And this notwithstanding the fact that he had twice given evidence against his American lessee, William Louis Winans. From which we can assume that Mackenzies' prime objective in distancing himself from Winans at the hearings was to divert public attention away from his own prime role in this notorious case. (17)

Not surprisingly, The 'Pet Lamb Case' became a *cause celebre,* and is one that is frequently referred to, down to this day, by the Ramblers' Association, and others, in the ongoing campaign for the right of access to mountains and moorland in all parts of Britain. For there can be no doubt that it illustrates the way all ordinary people, local, or visitors, suffer from the arbitrary exclusion of people from vast areas by a wealthy, medieval minority

42

of landowners. Notwithstanding these attitudes (which persist down to the present day) rambling, tourism and mountaineering have now overtaken the place occupied by deer stalking, grouse shooting and fly fishing in the economy of Scotland in general, and the Highlands in particular.

Today, thousands visit the Kintail and Glenshiel area every year. And many will, undoubtedly, be people of Scottish descent who will, in most cases, be fully aware of the sad history of the Highlanders under the still existing, medieval system of land ownership and tenure. Which, system, unfortunately, continues to distort the social and economic fabric of Scotland, and, indeed, the rest of the U.K.

Land reform being discussed at a village pub in 1892

Murdo Macrae died on 5th November 1903, aged 78. He left very little. (18)   The same, however, cannot be said for William Louis Winans and his brother Thomas. Thomas died on 10th June 1878 at the city of Newport, in the United States. In England alone he left a personal estate of just under £120,000. (19) William Louis Winans, one-time 'Monarch of the Scottish Glens' however, left considerably more when he died at his home, 10 Pembridge square, London, on 22 June, 1897.   The total sum was £2,522,005. (20) What his fortune would have been had he not wasted so much time and money enthusiastically chasing deer and Highland crofters it is impossible to calculate, but one imagines it would have been considerably more. What we do know for certain is that at the time of his death his other home in Great Britain was – and perhaps wisely so – at 1 Chichester Terrace, Brighton.   Which place, on reflection, is about as far away from irate Scottish Highlanders as one can possibly get in these overcrowded islands.

Murdo Macrae had his well-earned moment of glory in court when he won his case against Winans.   Sadly, though not surprisingly, the medieval system of land ownership remained firmly in place. The prime consideration, so far as the Lairds were concerned, was, of course, to secure an income that would allow them to maintain a standard of living they had grown accustomed to. And this invariably included a house in London. Also, and most importantly, membership of an exclusive London Club, and enough to send one's sons and heirs to Eton and Cambridge. And if this could only be achieved by driving fellow Scots off the land, well, so be it!

After the middle years of the 19th century, sad to say, the letting of shooting right in the Highlands became even more general. The catastrophic decline in the value of wool in 1874, and of sheep, ten years later, had a marked effect on large sheep farms, which, in turn, put more pressure on the poor, under-capitalised crofters. At the same time there was a steadily increasing demand for deer forests by wealthy shooting enthusiasts, of whom Winans was just a prime example.

As already noted, coinciding with this new source of income for the Scottish land-barons, was the arrival of the Victorian tourists, ramblers and mountaineers. And this started a still unresolved conflict of interest between the aforementioned, who came to the Highlands, to ramble, climb or tour, and those who wished to maintain their feudal hold on the land by keeping the mountains and moors free from such 'intruders' for the exclusive use of the gun-slinging fraternity. The point to appreciate here is that whilst visitors boosted the fragile Highland economy as a whole, the revenue they brought in did not necessarily go directly, or exclusively, into the over-stuffed back pockets of the medieval land barons.

But the pressure on the crofters, and Highlanders in general, increased. Their conditions at last attracting Parliamentary attention, firstly through the Commission of 1883, the subject of attention in this chapter, and again in 1892, which were both set up to inquire and report back to Parliament. Of particular significance is the fact that both these Commissions – even as the shooting enthusiast and author, Alexander Inkson McConnochie had to concede in 1923 – recommended that a check should be put on the spread of deer forests. (21) Again, no real action followed the production of these excellent Commission Reports. In practice matters became even worse!

Reading the 'Riot Act' to crofters opposing the land laws.
Isle of Lewis – January 1888

Crofters of Lewis in combat with police and marines.
Isle of Lewis – January 1888

In 1883 the Commissioners established that 1,975,209 acres of Scotland were being used exclusively as deer forests. (22) Almost unbelievably, however, at the time of the 1892 Inquiry the compilers had to report that the dear forest area of Scotland had risen to 2,472,133 acres. But notwithstanding these two damning reports, the forest area had increased again to 3,584,966 acres by 1912. A large part of an entire nation was being deliberately de-populated to make room for deer – and all for the benefit of the Lairds and their wealthy patrons! Reference should also be made on this subject to the report of the committee appointed in November 1919. That report (cmd. 1636) was issued in 1922, from which we can see that in 1920 the total acreage under deer was 3,432,385, which, of course, shows an insignificant drop from the 1912 figure. This, no doubt, due to the effects of the 1914–1918 World War, rather than any change of land policy. (23)

Nevertheless, the first Crofters Act did become law in 1885, following the publication of the first Commission report, but it offered only a mild, insignificant solution, for relatively few people. For instance, it offered no protection to the cottars, because, having no land, they were – and quite deliberately – not covered by its terms of reference. And, needless to say, the vast majority of the land remained firmly in the hands of Scotland's land barons – where it remains down to the present day.

It was, however, against the immediate background of the 1883 Report of the Commissioners that James Bryce MP, doyen of the British rambling and mountaineering movements, tabled his famous Bill to secure to the public access to mountains and moorland in Scotland. Bryce's life-style was far removed from the hard, punishing existence of the Highland cottar, Murdo Macrae, and Bryce's aims were also more limited. Nevertheless, in their respective ways both men were holding aloft banners calling for the same thing – freedom from domination by oppressive landowners!

And for this they have entered the pages of British history with honour and distinction.

The gunboat *Jackal,* at Loch Luirbost – sent north to quell the rioting crofters of Lewis in 1888. The crofters involved were all supporters of the radical "Land League."

CHAPTER FOUR   JAMES BRYCE & THE ACCESS BILLS

The year of 1884 was a remarkable one in British history. In January Major-General Charles G. Gordon, suppressor of the Taeping Rebellion, was making his way to the Sudan as the accredited agent of the British Government. When Gordon was preparing to make his way up the Nile, where he was destined to take his historic stand against the powerful Mahdi at Khartoum, James Bryce MP was making his final preparations to take a stand against the powerful Scottish landowners.

As a great rambler and mountaineer, James Bryce already had first hand experience of the restrictions to access that existed in Scotland. Of equal importance, however, was the fact that he was friendly with many of the people in London who had just fought with much success to save the commons and open spaces in and around the capital. Not surprisingly, one of the first things he resolved to do on entering Parliament was to fight for freedom of access in the Scottish Highlands.

His famous Access to Mountains (Scotland) Bill was introduced on 28th February 1884. Later in the same year the Government was to publish 'The Report of the Royal Commissioners of Inquiry on the Condition of Crofters and Cottars in the Highlands of Scotland.' This publication, with many others, spotlighted the already mentioned fact that vast deer forests covered much of the Highlands, tenants were being persecuted and tourists were being vigorously discouraged from entering these exclusive hunting and shooting domains.

Although quite clearly mindful of all these factors and, one does not doubt sympathetic to the Crofter's cause, it is interesting to note that Bryce made no *obvious* attempt to link the 'Access' issue with the Crofters struggles, although both issues were clearly complementary. He, no doubt, reasoned that he stood a better chance of winning support for his Bill if he did not identify access with the even more radical fight for survival being mounted by the crofters against the landowners. He would also have been aware that many prominent fellow liberals were also landowners, and keen sportsmen! But firstly, let us take a brief glance at Bryce himself.

Viscount James Bryce (1838–1922), jurist, rambler, mountaineer, historian and politician, was born 10th May 1838 in Arthur Street, Belfast. In 1846 he moved with his parents to Glasgow. In 1854 he entered Glasgow University, where he studied Greek, and also obtained a prize in mathematics. In 1863 he went on to study history at Oxford. It was, however, when he was at Glasgow University that he acquired an interest in botany and a taste for climbing.

This taste for climbing endured in later life, and he pursued it in many far-away places. He climbed several peaks in the Alps and Dolomites, he ascended Hekla in Iceland in 1872, the Maladetta and the Vignemale in the Pyrenees in 1873, and Mount Ararat in 1878. A member of (Sir) Leslie Stephen's celebrated London-based mountaineering and rambling group, 'The Sunday Tramps', in 1878 Bryce, with Stephens, ascended the Tatra Ridge in the Carpathians.

1. The peak of Schiehallion, seen from the Bifurcation of the Tummel River. 2. The woods of Crossmount, and Peak of Schiehallion from the gorge below the terraces of Dunalastair. 3. Village of Kinloch Rannoch, Loch Rannoch in the distance. 4. Iron bridge over the River Tummel. 5. Valley of the Tummel from Crossmount Woods, Loch Rannoch in the distance. 6. Falls of the Tummel, Dunalastain.

Views in the Vale of Rannoch, Scotland, in 1884, when James Bryce introduced the Access to Mountains (Scotland) Bill

Bryce also climbed in Hawaii, Basutoland, Italy and Japan. In 1879 he was elected a member of the Alpine Club, of which he was president from 1899 to 1901. In 1898 he was greatly honoured in North America when the triple-peaked Mount Bryce of the Canadian Rockies was named after him. (1)

Of greater significance, so far as Scotland is concerned, however, is the fact that in 1887 the 'Cairngorm Club' was founded, and The Rt. Hon. James Bryce, D.C.L., M.P. was elected to serve as this famous mountaineering club's first president. Alex. Inkson M'Connochie of Aberdeen was the first Secretary. W.M. Gilbert of *The Scotsman* was a member, and although a large percentage of the members came from Aberdeen, and other parts of Scotland, it is interesting to note that the membership list also included Jaakoff Prelooker of Odessa, C.A. Su-Vong, of Banchory-Devenick and Sir Wm. Wedderburn, Bart MP from Gloucester. (2)

In 1880 Bryce entered Parliament as Liberal member for Tower Hamlets. He was to serve as an MP for 26 years. At the election of 1885 he did not stand again for Tower Hamlets, but was elected for South Aberdeen, and held the seat until 1907. Though professionally inexperienced in diplomacy, he was appointed by Sir Henry Campbell-Bannerman as Ambassador to the United States, a post which he held for six eventful years. (3)

James Bryce, Regius Professor of Civil Law and MP for South
Aberdeen, c 1885

It was, however, when James Bryce came to London that he took an already well-established interest in rambling to a decidedly more advanced level. This he did by joining the very challenging ranks of 'The Sunday Tramps', the exclusive, London-based rambling group, of whom Leslie Stephens was the guide. There can have been few roads or paths within a thirty mile radius from the capital, which were not familiar to him.

During the same period he also joined with others in the ongoing campaign to preserve open spaces and footpaths, in or near the capital, from the inroads of developers and landowners. Such matters he frequently brought to the attention of Parliament when serving as member for Tower Hamlets. But above all Bryce was anxious to ensure that the wild and rugged beauty of his native Scotland were open to all, by removing the bans which had been placed upon open access to the grouse moors and deer forests by the imperious dictates of sport.

Not surprisingly, however, Bryce immediately encountered polite but massive opposition from those with a vested interest in hunting and shooting. The main trouble was and, as already noted, the shooting of deer and grouse had become incredibly 'fashionable.' To own, or even be a lessee of a deer forest or a grouse moor was seen as the coveted symbol of social and business success. Shootings were being let at fancy prices, and Southern, and even Transatlantic wealth, via men such as Winans was flowing into the pockets of the Scottish Lairds. As one they argued that the value of their forests would be severely depreciated if tourists were made free to roam over it at will and frighten the deer during the stalking season. (4) Undaunted, however, James Bryce introduced his famous Bill. The preamble read:

"Whereas large tracts of uncultivated mountain and moor land in Scotland, formerly depastured by sheep and cattle, have of late years been stocked with deer, and attempts have been made to deprive Her Majesty's subjects of the rights which they have heretofore enjoyed of walking upon these and other tracts of uncultivated mountain and moor land for purposes of recreation and scientific or artistic study, subject to proper provision for preventing any abuse of such rights." (5)

Naturally, Parliament dismissed the Bill – without debate! Nevertheless, the general public had much sympathy for Bryce, all of which was reflected in a favourable article, published in *The Times* soon after the Bill had been introduced. It began:

"Under the quaint title, Access to Mountains (Scotland) Bill, Mr Bryce has introduced a Bill which, quite apart from its chances of success, will have a certain scientific value. That value is in social statics; that is, in the comparative strength of various forces now moving and ultimately forming the national character. What is the comparative weight of numbers, and of money or rank? The Sportsman is a survival of prehistoric times. The lover of the picturesque is a creature of modern civilisation, inasmuch that some have doubted whether he existed, in classical antiquity."

The article then went on to point out that every year many thousands were making their way north to Scotland in quest of scenery which was quite as beautiful as Switzerland, but they were invariably warned by the guide books to keep away from many routes, due to the fact that they would be confronted "with a fortifications of strong fences, locked gates, resolute gamekeepers, men of action, and the terrors of the law". Then, to make matters absolutely clear, the writer stated that up against the multitude of tourists, were the tiny minority who went North to shoot grouse or stalk deer. The radical writer then added:

"Practically, grouse and red deer are worthless, or of scarcely appreciable value. It is for the glory of saying that they have made such a bag, or killed so many head, that they pay a rent of hundreds and thousands for a shooting. The pecuniary result is a largely increased rental, which, though received by Scotch proprietors, is not generally spent in Scotland. Here, then, are two opposing armies: the tourists on the one side, and the renters and letters of shooting on the other."

The writer then concluded in a manner that was radical, but most reasonable. He called for a 'compromise' on the issue, and by doing so avoided making any too disturbing a challenge to the medieval rights of large-scale land barons.

"Is it not a matter for compromise! Surely the lords of the soil cannot claim so absolute a monopoly of earth's surface, and of the most beautiful parts of it, as wholly to shut out the poor holiday folk, the artist, and the naturalist. Surely the many have rights as well as the few, and they that wish to see are entitled legislative protection as much as they that wish to kill also. On the other hand, numbers cannot claim utterly to destroy the rights of property; that is, the right to some exclusive use of it. The problem cannot be insoluble." (6)

It is clear, however, that Bryce's membership of the Cairngorm Club increased his resolve to press ahead on the issue of access to mountain and moorland. He did, once more, in February 1888, when he tried again by presenting a further Bill, which followed the first one word for word. Unfortunately, in a Government largely composed of 'Sporting' landowners, it failed to receive serious consideration.

Nevertheless, just two months later, in April of the same year, a like-minded access champion for Wales spoke up in the House. This was Tom Ellis, MP for Merionethshire, with his even more radical Mountains, Rivers and Pathways (Wales) Bill, which added to the list of reasonable access demands already made. "The free right of the public to have access to or walk along the bed or bank of any stream, or lake, to ride in any boat, coracle or canoe upon any river or lake, for the purpose of recreation, wimberry gathering, sketching or antiquarian research". Sadly, but predictably, Tom Ellis' Bill also failed to gain support in the House. (7)

Unfortunately, the only time that Bryce actually managed to secure a debate on Access was in March 1892, when he submitted a motion in favour of an Access to Mountains Bill. He stated that there was a great deal of misunderstanding with regards to the proposal. It was not, he added, directed against sport or sporting. All he asked was that he was allowed to bring forward and present to the House the grievance and suffering caused to the people of the United Kingdom by their exclusion from their right to enjoy the scenery of their own country.

Bryce then made the significant point that complaints were then most numerous respecting the country round Braemar which, of course, is close to the royal estate of Balmoral, acquired by Prince Albert for the Royal Family in 1848. And although Bryce was too diplomatic to actually identify the proprietors by name he skilfully aimed verbal broadsides at them in his long opening speech:

"Braemar, however, is one of those places where the process of sealing up the country is carried furthest. It is hardly possible to stir off the roads in the neighbourhood of Braemar without being confronted by a ghillie, and threatened with proceedings by interdict. Even those superb mountains between the source of the Dee and the valley of the Spey are so closed that one is obliged to stalk ghillies as the ghillies stalk the deer." (8)

57

Heading out to a Royal Hunt in the Highlands in 1880

The debate of 1892 on Access was a long one, which culminated in Bryce successfully carrying a resolution that legislation was needed. But when, in the following session, he tried to give this practical effect by introducing a Bill, he was defeated by the conservative ministry, who stated that they intended to bring in a Bill themselves. As might be expected, however, their proposals, when tabled, proved very disappointing. Primarily, because this very devious Bill deliberately exempted the very months when people visited the Highlands! Understandably, Bryce, the champion of Access to Mountains, quite rightly declined to accept it. (9)

Undaunted, Bryce soldiered on, submitting an Access Bill for the last time in 1898, which, once again, was rejected. (10) But the struggle continued. In February 1900, Bryce's younger brother, Annan, presented the same Access Bill, and did so again in 1906, 1908, and 1909, but each time without success. Over the next thirty years nine Access Bills were presented, all more or less the same as Bryce's original Bill. A notable one of these being Thompson's Access to Mountains Bill of 1924, which was supported by Dr. Ernest A Baker, the well-known mountaineer, author, and champion of open access to mountain and moorland.

In a letter to *The Times* supporting Thompson's Bill, Baker made the point that there were signs that some Highland landowners were no longer blind to the evil's of the present system, and were thus prepared for a reasonable compromise. Many, according to Baker, admitted that the glens should again be used for small scale farming, and the mountain sides for forestry, and that water power and other sources should be developed. (11)

However, in this chapter, which is, primarily, a tribute to James Bryce, I think it would be appropriate to conclude by quoting from the speech he made when arguing the case for his Access Bill in 1892. As his biographer, H.A.L. Fisher put it in 1927: "The speech ended with a burst of true but unparliamentary eloquence such as does not often startle the ear of the British legislature."

"Man does not live by bread alone. The Creator speaks to his creatures through his works, and appointed the grandeur and loveliness of the mountains and glens and the silence of the moorlands lying open under the eye of the heaven, to have their fitting influence on the thoughts of men. Stirring their nature and touching their imagination, chasing away cares and the dull monotony of everyday life and opening up new and inexhaustible sources of enjoyment and delight. It is on behalf of these enjoyments and those who need them most and in the hope of preserving for the people one of the most precious parts of their national heritage that I ask the House to agree this resolution." (12)

CHAPTER FIVE
THE COMMONS PRESERVATION SOCIETY

Meanwhile, in London and the Home Counties, hundreds of miles to the south of Scotland, work was in hand in the 1860's to preserve our common lands. This brought into existence The Commons Preservation Society, as it was then called. It became the Commons, Open Spaces and Footpath Preservation Society in 1894, a change brought about by a merger with the National Footpath Preservation Society.

Operating today as The Open Spaces Society it is now Britain's oldest conservation organisation. Founded on 19th July 1866 by Lord Eversley, with a group of friends who supported the group's aims and objectives, it was soon joined by other eminent people who all added their weight to the cause. (1) Founding and early members include Sir Robert Hunter, Sir Lawrence Wensley Chubb, Miss Octavia Hill, Canon Rawnsley, George Grote, James Bryce, John Stuart Mill, Edward North Buxton, Henry Fawcett, and [Sir] Lesley Stephen – founder of the 'Sunday Tramps.' Eversley, Hunter, Chubb, and Hill, of course, were the most active of these early members. Accordingly, a glance at the life and times of these four individuals will help to put the work of the society into proper perspective.

Baron Eversley was the only son of Sir George Shaw-Lefevre, and nephew of Charles Shaw-Lefevre, Viscount Eversley. Educated at Eton and Cambridge, he took his degree in 1853. In the same year he visited the slave market at Richmond, Virginia where he viewed with disgust the slave system in operation. He was elected as the Liberal member for Reading in 1863. His maiden speech, delivered in 1864, was clearly influenced by his visit to Virginia in 1853. He expressed a then unfashionable sympathy for Lincoln and the North in the American Civil War. He pleaded that the *Alabama,* then being built at the Laird yard in Birkenhead, for the pro-slavery Confederacy, should not be allowed to leave the Mersey.

His third speech, delivered in 1865, was aimed at establishing public rights over all commons. This was the cause for which he contended all his life, and he had the satisfaction in 1925 of seeing it embodied in a statute, although even then it only applied to commons in urban districts. It was, to an appreciable extent, due to the work of Eversley, and the Society he established, that England owes the preservation, from the enclosing landlord and the encroaching builder, of Hampstead Heath, Epping Forest, and many other famous commons. (2)

Kate Ashbook has recently drawn our attention to the fact that: "One of the Society's first battles was to save Hampstead Heath from being excavated for sand and gravel. Also, in 1866, when Lord Brownlow erected two miles of iron railings around Berkhamstead Common in Hertfordshire, the society organised a trainload of navvies from Euston to Tring. They walked the two miles to the common and pulled down the fencing at dead of night. It was never replaced and now Berkhamstead Common belongs to the National Trust and is open to all". (3)

On the question of 'Direct Action' – as in the above case – Howard Hill has also reminded us, and without wishing to detract in any way from the work of Lord Eversley and other members of the society, the most important role in preserving our commons was continually played by thousands of ordinary people who took direct action to halt the enclosures. For example, and as Lord Eversley readily concedes in his book, it was the mass protest against the savage treatment meted out to three labourers, arrested and jailed for lopping trees in Epping Forest, that was largely responsible for it being saved. He records how, on 10 November 1879, five to six thousand people turned out to exercise *their* right to lop trees. An act of solidarity which, it is pleasant to record, eventually compelled those responsible to return 3,000 acres to the public. The opening ceremony took place on 11th March 1882, at which notable event Queen Victoria declared the forest open to the public without "let or hindrance.". (4)

Firs near North End

The Old taverns

Sketches on Hampstead Heath, 1871

Epping Forest – view from High Beech - 1884

Sir Robert Hunter (1844–1913) solicitor and noted authority on commons and public rights of way was born in London on 27th October 1844. He was educated at London University. After taking his MA in 1865 he studied law and was admitted a solicitor in 1867. As already noted, public opinion was then being stirred at that time by the enclosure of many metropolitan commons, and notably by Sir Henry Peak, of Wimbledon, who was offering prizes on the subject. Hunter completed his essay, and gained a prize. This led to Hunter becoming a partner in the firm of Fawcett, Horne, and Hunter in 1869. The firm then became the official solicitors to the Commons Preservation Society.

And it was Hunter who was then entrusted with the conduct of the suits that led to the protection of Hampstead Heath, Berkhamstead, Plumstead and Wimbledon commons, and other threatened open spaces. He also established the principles on which the law relating to commons is now based. The most notable case he was involved in was concerning the aforementioned recovery of 3,000 acres of Epping Forest.

Hunter's interest in the movement for protecting commons was maintained, and until his death he remained closely identified with the Commons Preservation Society. In 1895, Hunter, with Miss Octavia Hill and Canon Rawnsley, founded the National Trust, which, today, is a national institution. He lived in Haslemere and was instrumental in preserving in that area over 1,500 acres of commons, including Hindhead, and the Devils Punchbowl. He retired early in 1913 and, rather sadly, died a few short months later on 6th November in the same year. As a national memorial to his work a woodland adjoining the Waggoner's Wells, near Hazlemere, was purchased by public subscription. (5)

Commons Preservation. Sketch of the prettiest corner of Barnes common, 1877

Sir Lawrence Wensley Chubb (1873–1948) was born in Australia on 21st December, 1873. His father was a prospector and mine owner of New South Wales. He returned to England with his parents in 1887. He completed his education in London at the Borough Polytechnic. Of interest to us is the fact that whilst studying at the Polytechnic his main recreation was exploring the nearby countryside on foot. He also joined the Polytechnic Debating Society, where he met Octavia Hill! On her recommendation, in 1894, he was appointed Secretary of the Kent and Surrey Committee of the Commons Preservation Society.

It was, of course, just one year later, in 1895, that Lawrence Chubb, with Octavia Hill, Canon Rawnsley, and others, formed the National Trust. Chubb became the Trust's first Secretary, but he only remained in this post for twelve months, at which point in time he became the Secretary of the Commons, Footpaths and Open Spaces Society. In 1905 Chubb, with others, founded the London-Based Ramblers' Federation, of which he was first secretary and later vice-president. He also involved himself in many other activities connected with sport and the protection of the countryside, which included acting as Secretary of the National Playing Fields Association, also work related to the establishment of Nature Reserves and National Parks.

Noted for his tact, and his ability as a negotiator, Chubb was, nevertheless, very much part of the 'Establishment.' He was, essentially, a conservative-minded late Victorian gentleman. Inevitably, therefore, there were many in the rambling movement who felt – and with considerable justification – that Chubb was too ready to compromise. A prime example of this surfaced in the 1930's when the 1939 Access to Mountains Act was under discussion.

One would like to think that the argument here was a simple one, between landowners, anxious to exclude, and ramblers seeking access. Unfortunately, as Tom Stephenson, leader of the Ramblers' Association felt obliged to point out, this was not the case. Namely, because the very suspect right-leaning 'compromise' that emerged in 1939 was, it would seem, 'stage-managed' from within the amenity movement by the undoubtedly capable, but conservative-minded, Sir Lawrence Chubb of the Commons Society!

What actually happened was that Geoffrey Manders, MP for Wolverhampton, presented an amended version of the 1939 Access to Mountains Bill to Parliament in which he advocated that access should be limited to just 9 months of the year. Fortunately, it never got very far, but this was the first intimation that the Ramblers' Association might have to go it alone in the fight for open access to mountain and moorland, without the wholehearted support of Chubb and the Commons Society. Manders, it seems, was under the influence of Chubb, which prompted Edwin Royce of the Ramblers' Association to pen the following lines to Manders:

"The entry of the Commons and Footpaths Society is regarded with misgivings by Northern ramblers and one Federation (West Riding) has already made a protest. The reasons are the propensity of the Society to make compromises with landowners, as it did in the case of the Rights of Way Act 1932 and the known antagonism of the Secretary, Sir Lawrence Chubb". (6)

Manders replied to Royce saying the action taken was a wise one, and that he thought Sir Lawrence was genuinely anxious to help. (7) The issue remains a controversial one. Nevertheless, leaving aside the 'Access' issue, it has to be acknowledged that in many other ways Sir Lawrence Chubb did make a very constructive contribution to the countryside movement, for which he should be remembered with respect. He died at his home in Richmond on 18th February 1948.

67

"No Thoroughfare"
"Trespassers will be prosecuted with the utmost rigour of the law"

"This little rustic incident shows a boy, boy-like, ready to explore forbidden ground in defiance of all authority, and a girl, girl-like, restraining him, from her feminine instinct of obedience. What mischief this little urchin would commit beyond plucking wild flowers or blackberry gathering we are not prepared to say; but to many who would certainly do no mischief at all. As, for example, artists on a sketching expedition – the threats of "prosecuting trespassers with the utmost vigour of the law are often sufficiently provoking." However, such threats are commonly disregarded, and very rarely is any attempt made to carry them into execution, except it may be by the vulgar millionaire, the *nouveau riche* overweeningly proud of his new character of landed proprietor. Almost invariably, the higher and older the family the more tolerant is the proprietor of intrusion on his domain." (?) (8)

Miss Octavia Hill (1838–1912) the great philanthropist, Christian Socialist, housing reformer, and founder member of the Commons Preservation Society and the National Trust, was born at Wisbech on the 3rd December 1838. She was the 8th daughter of James Hill, corn merchant and banker, who was noted locally for his good work in municipal and educational reform. Her mother was Caroline Southwood Smith, daughter of Dr. Thomas Southwood Smith, the well-known expert on fever epidemics and sanitation. Octavia, with several of her younger sisters, was educated at home by her mother. About 1852, when she was just fourteen years old, she began work in London for an organisation known as the 'Ladies Guild', a co-operative association promoted by the Christian Socialists. Her mother soon became manager of this group. Octavia's work with the exceptionally poor, and the influence of the Christian Socialists shaped her character and outlook.

Another decisive influence in determining the direction of Octavia's life was her association with the 'Laker' John Ruskin, whom she first met in 1853. Soon after this she became deeply involved in the housing problems of the poor and, in 1864, succeeded in interesting Ruskin in her schemes for improving the dwellings of poor working class people in London. She was, in fact, instrumental in establishing the present day 'Housing Association' movement, and in this she was eternally grateful to Ruskin for putting up the capital to purchase the first properties for her association.

But Octavia Hill was much more than a housing reformer. Her struggle for the preservation of open spaces and footpaths was remarkable. In the closing decades of the 19th century, as already noted, commons and open spaces in or near London, were under threat by the construction industry. Without hesitation Octavia, with many others, some of whom have already been mentioned, threw herself into the ongoing movement to save such places. Her invaluable work for the Commons Preservation Society was a vital part of this ongoing task. (9)

The foregoing gives an indication of the calibre of the founding members of the Commons Preservation Society, as it was then called. Lord Eversley, in particular, had 'political clout' for his father was the Speaker of the House of Commons, all of which helped! However, and as already mentioned, Eversley was the first to point out that thousands of ordinary working people had also played their part in securing rights of way and protecting common lands. Eversley was also fair and objective enough to concede that his Association had not been the first for dealing with commons in the interest of the general public.

He also drew attention to the fact that at the opposite end of the social spectrum some aristocratic members of society had also played a positive role in this movement, among whom, in 1864, was the then Earl Spencer, forebear of the late Diana, Princess of Wales! The movement he was involved in was one of the first to be set up in Britain, and it arose in respect of Wimbledon Common – one of the largest, most beautiful, and best valued of all such places in the London area. A full year before the Commons Preservation Society was established, Earl Spencer, Lord of the Manor of Wimbledon, announced his intention to dedicate the greater part of this Common to the public.

The upshot of this was that a private Bill was laid before Parliament, which related to the sale of about one third of the area of the common. The proceeds of this sale were then expended on buying up and extinguishing any rights which the commoners had over the common, and fencing, draining and improving the remaining 680 acres. The public park thus created, as distinguished from an open common, was then vested in the hands of responsible trustees. (10)

Another famous 'Open Space' is Burham Beeches, near Slough, and just 25 miles from London. Since the late 1870's it has been very popular with ramblers and day-trippers from the metropolis. Here, it is interesting to record, it was saved from the builders by the direct intervention of the London City Corporation, who voted 'a moderate sum' to purchase "this remnant of Sylvan beauty". (11)

A picnic at Burnham Beeches, near Slough, in 1879

Throughout the last decades of the 19th and the early decades of the 20th centuries the work of the Society continued. In 1932, after the formation of the various Ramblers' Federations, and prior to the establishment of the Ramblers' Association in 1935, the Open Spaces Society was still playing the leading role in the struggle to save commons and footpaths – a fact acknowledged in *The Ramblers Yearbook* for 1933, the official organ of the Liverpool and District Ramblers' Federation.

In an article about the Society, A.L. Simpson, the Assistant General Secretary, reported that at the Societies Annual Conference, held early in 1932, most of the Ramblers' Federations had sent representatives where the need for new cross-country routes by footpath and bridleway was discussed at great length. Simpson then paid tribute to the ongoing work of the Society and the Federations. "An outstanding feature of the years work has been the steady growth in the number of rural commons whose owners have placed their land under the protection of Section 193 of the Law of Property Act, which gives to the public the right of access to them for air and exercise." (12)

Today, the General Secretary of the Open Spaces Society is Kate Ashbrook, who also sits on the Ramblers' Association Executive Committee. She has played a leading role in campaigning for the recently introduced Countryside and Right of Way Act, and continues to dedicate herself to this cause, until all matters concerning this Act are implemented. The Society is also leading the campaign for a new law for common land, which is a large task for a small organisation to undertake.

THE ADVANTAGES OF OUR SUBURBS

"What I like about a residence in the Suburbs is the walks you can get, you know!" (1878)

CHAPTER SIX   THE SUNDAY TRAMPS

The last decades of the 19th Century saw the establishment of the first organised rambling clubs. Invariably male-dominated, these late Victorian gentlemen's clubs also tended to be socially exclusive. All members had to be nominated and 'vetted' prior to acceptance into the hallowed ranks. Almost without exception, the members would be drawn from the ranks of the urban, upper middle classes. In short, the literary and academic, legal and political circles of the period. The same period also saw the establishment of many mountaineering clubs. On which point, one should note, many of these pioneer 'rambling clubs' also featured serious mountaineering and challenging cave exploration on their 'walks' programme! Further to this even the 'walks' listed often seemed to have more in common with a training programme for the Olympic Games, than common-or-garden rambling.

Without a doubt, however, the most famous, exclusive (and influential) of all such clubs was the London-based 'Sunday Tramps', founded by [Sir] Leslie Stephen on 2nd November 1879. Among its elite band of members were the novelist and poet George Meredith, Professor Frederick William Maitland, Arthur John Butler, Viscount Haldane, and the Trevelyans, father and son, both of whom were destined to play leading roles in the 'Out-O-Doors' movement of the early twentieth century.

Sir Leslie Stephen (1832–1904) the founder of the 'Sunday Tramps' and the first editor of *The Dictionary of National Biography,* was born in London on the 28th November 1832. He was the son of Sir James Stephen and his mother, Jane Catherine, the daughter of John Venn, the well-known evangelical rector of Clapham. In the autumn of 1840 the Stephen family moved down to Brighton for the sake of young Leslie's health, for he was then thought to be suffering from what must surely be an exceptionally rare malady with school pupils – a precociously active brain! In

1847 he was sent to King's College London then, after some coaching, he entered Trinity Hall in 1850. To the university Leslie Stephen owes a great debt, for up to this point his health was decidedly fragile, but at Trinity he improved dramatically.

This improvement was so marked that he was soon 'spontaneously drawn to athletics' to which activity he was previously indifferent. To the extent that he became a noted long-distance runner, a walker of exceptional endurance and an almost fanatical oarsman. His 'staying-power' soon became almost legendary. For example, on one notable occasion he walked from Cambridge to dine in London, fifty miles in twelve hours! Then, in 1860, he won the mile race (five minutes, four seconds) at the university athletic games. (1)

Impressive as the above achievements are, it was really as a mountaineer that his athletic zeal showed to best advantage. In 1855 he tramped through the Bavarian Highlands and, in 1857 with Francis Galton, he made his first Swiss ascent of the Col du Geant. The following year, after conquering Monte Rosa, Leslie Stephen joined the famous Alpine Club. [In July 1865 the great Alpinist, Edward Whymper, made his ill-fated climb of the Matterhorn, when four of the seven strong party fell to their deaths.] A year later, as already noted, Leslie Stephen spent the summer of 1866 in the Carpathians with James Bryce. (2)

Leslie Stephen and party ascending the Rothhorn

The 'Sunday Tramps' was established, quite informally by Leslie Stephen after his second marriage to Julia Prinsep, in March 1878. Events leading up to the founding of the group are as follows. Leslie Stephen, with George Croom Robertson, Professor of Mental Philosophy and editor of *Mind*, had been editing papers in collaboration with the noted scholar, Sir Frederick Pollock. Late in 1879 these three men, together with a few companions, arranged to go on long rambles in the countryside every other Sunday. The original members of the society were about ten in number, all of whom had an interest in philosophy, but in the course of time most professions [not trades!] were represented. (3)

Leslie Stephen, the academic with a fine record as a mountain climber had, by this time, given up risky mountain ascents, but he was still very active. It was this factor which prompted him to take fortnightly walks in the country with a small band of close friends. Organised and led by Stephen, the members were also most carefully selected by him. The standing arrangement was to walk on every other Sunday for about six months of the year. The usual aim of the leader was to organise a cross-country walk from one railway to another. Attractive scenery in the hilly and heath-land areas of Kent and Surrey, together with trips to the more picturesque stretches of the Thames Valley, featured prominently in the selection. (4)

Stephen showed great skill in planning the routes, and also for discovering short cuts not indicated by the maps. This, in real terms, meant trespassing, which brought the eminent members of this group, representing the rapidly expanding ranks of the urban bourgeoisie, into direct conflict with the perceived interests of the established, often aristocratic, land-owning elite. Speaking about this issue, many years later, in January, 1930, one of the founder members stated:

"They [The Sunday Tramps] avoided high roads and trespassed, if necessary, discreetly over private property in their pursuit of short cuts or the fairest bits of the countryside. And it is due to the ingenuity of Sir Frederick Pollack, acting we believe, on a hint from no less an authority than Lord Bramwell, that the following legal formula was invented for the Tramps when called upon to deal with troublesome gamekeeper or owner presuming to warn them off his property: "We hereby give you notice that we do not, nor doth any of us, claim any right of way or other easement into or over these lands, and we tender you this shilling by way of amends. It should be noted that this formula is most effective when repeated, after the leader, in solemn chant by a large party of Tramps." (5)

Arrested for trespassing. The hazards of rambling in 1884

[Under the title of "Our Walking Tour" the illustrations on the previous page are the concluding part of an item which appeared in the *Illustrated London News,* in September 1884. The periodical's talented artist, E. Morant Cox, may well have had the Tramps in mind when he produced it!]

Leslie Stephen, of course, set the pace on the actual walks. Notably, by regularly opting for serious 'Combat Grade' route marches! On which point, it has to be said, he invariably found it difficult, if not impossible, to allow for the walking limitations of lesser mortals. For instance, the catching of a train at the end of one of his twenty-mile long endurance tests, often obliged the tail end of his long-suffering party to break into a run. Lunch on these rambles was usually enjoyed in a humble pub; the meaner-looking the Inn, the more Stephen seemed to like it, for he had not named his group the 'Sunday Tramps' without due consideration. Bread and cheese and a pint of beer was the standard repast, and there was indeed very rarely any other fare on the menu in those less sophisticated days. (6)

However, as well as enjoying humble pub lunches the 'Sunday Tramps' would, on occasion, be invited to a well-earned lunch or afternoon tea at Stephen's home. Among other hospitable homes open to them was Charles Darwin's at Down, and George Meredith's at Box Hill.

The following canticle, written by Arthur John Butler, one of the founder members of the group, recalls the spirit of the membership, as it was in those distant, pre-coach and car days, well over one hundred years ago.

THE BALLADE OF THE SUNDAY TRAMPS

"If weary you grow at your books
    Or Dyspeptical after you've dined
If your wife makes remarks on your looks,
    If in short you feel somewhat inclined
    For fresh air and a six mile grind
And good metaphysical talk –
    With a party of writers in Mind
You should go for a Sabbath day's walk.

Leave the town by the earliest train
    (In your Bradshaw betimes underlined)
With umbrella in case it should rain,
    Enduring the sun and the wind –
    'Tis no harm if they toughen your rind –
Your boots you'll remember to caulk,
    Your pockets with sandwiches lined,
You are good for a twenty-mile walk.

Though surely we all by our rule
    Are as peripatetics defined,
Yet each philosophical school
    Is here with each other combined:
    Idealists, realists, find
Representatives here, as we stalk
    In the breezes, like them unconfined,
Over hills of clay, gravel or chalk.

So, Prince, leave your troubles behind,
    And resolving for one day to baulk
Black care, with rivers in Mind
    Go forth for your Sabbath day's walk.
                A.J.B., April 3rd 1881" (7)

Kitchen of the 'Walnut Tree Inn' Adlington, Kent in 1885. Typical of the pubs used by the The 'Sunday Tramps' during this period

The 'Sunday Tramps' – in it's first phase of existence – was in being for fifteen years, and during this period the total number of names in Stephen's book was sixty, together with one 'corresponding member' – Professor Vinogradoff, of Moscow. But at any one time there was never more than about twenty active members, and if ten actually turned out for a walk this was considered a good assembly. In 1891 Leslie Stephen resigned as leader. Pollock took his place, except during intervals when R.G. Marsden and Douglas Freshfield took charge of the group.

The last walk made by members of the old fraternity was taken in March 1895. They were down, but not out, for the group revived in the early years of the 20th century with the blessing of Pollock and other founder members. The great historian, George Macaulay Trevelyan, then became a prominent member of the 'Born-Again' team. (8) In January 1930 a special dinner was held to celebrate the establishment of the group over 50 years ago in 1878. On this notable occasion Sir Frederick Pollock, who was present on the first ramble, took the chair.

From his speech it emerged that in March 1895 it was recorded in the original journal that "the numbers not being sufficient, the walks were suspended." However, they were revived just nine years later by the sons of the first two members, Toby Stephen and John Pollock. And since then, Pollock stated, the 'Tramps' had never ceased walking together and, as before, in the vicinity of London. Interestingly, by this time an offshoot of the 'Tramps' had been established in Montreal, which group sent a cable to those at the dinner containing best wishes to the parent body. (9)

Many members of the 'Sunday Tramps' were also active members of the famous 'Alpine Club'. In addition to Leslie Stephen and James Bryce, their numbers included the following, Professor Arthur John Butler, Professor Frederick William Maitland, international banker, Sir Felix Otto Schuster, who died at Ruthin Castle, Denbigh, in May 1936, Douglas William Freshfield, famous mountain explorer, and one time President of the Alpine Club, and Professor Sir Frederick Pollock. (10) Which indicates that they were all active in the 'Alpine Club', alongside the most famous of all 'Alpine Club' members – Edward Whymper. A short tribute to him at this point is, therefore, in a very real sense, also a tribute to his colleagues from the 'Sunday Tramps' walking group.

Whymper's most remarkable experience was in July, 1865, when climbing on the Matterhorn in a party headed by Lord Francis Douglas. The rope broke, and four of the seven-strong team fell to their deaths. This terrible disaster gave Whymper a European reputation in connection with the Matterhorn. (11) After an action-packed life he died at Chamonix on 16th September 1911. It was then that the people of this Alpine village paid their respects to him, which they did quietly, and with great dignity. The scene was graphically described by his biographer, F.S. Smythe:

"On the morning of the funeral two guides knocked at every door in the village and said, "Edward Whymper will be buried here today, and you are asked to attend his funeral at 2.30 this afternoon". The summons was obeyed and all Chamonix turned out to pay their respects. A party of guides carried the coffin, and the pall bearers included representatives of various clubs, and Frederick Payout, who had assisted in the search for the victims of the Matterhorn disaster.

"The fine weather had broken. New snow lay on the mountainsides, vividly white beneath a roof of sullen cloud through which glaciers thrust their green tongues. The air was very still. There was no sound save for the gritting of nailed boots on the rocky path to the cemetery, finer music to Whymper's ears, could he have heard it, than the grandest requiem. In this way, simply, peacefully, and appropriately, passed Edward Whymper." (12)

A 'Fog Bow' as seen from the Matterhorn by Edward Whymper, and his fellow-survivors, soon after the disaster on that mountain on 14th July 1865

CHAPTER SEVEN
PIONEER RAMBLING CLUBS 1874–1900

The establishment of our pioneering rambling clubs, in the second part of the 19th century, was set against a traumatic social background which we should, perhaps, take note first. Ever since the rural workers had lost their land, vast numbers had been forced to move to the large industrial cities, or sail to the colonies. The impact of industrial and agricultural developments was now hitting the rural poor with brutal force. Working conditions on the land were at an all-time low. The 'Potato Famine' had hit Ireland, in particular, a terrible blow in the 1840's, but many other parts of the British Isles were also struck with great force by this terrible series of crop failures. All of which greatly accelerated a sad exodus from our countryside to the dubious haven offered by our 19th century industrial towns.

However, Britain, under Queen Victoria, was now becoming a great manufacturing country and work, of some sort, was to be found for men and women in the great cities, towns and ports. Invariably, men would walk to the urban areas in an effort to find work and accommodation. If they succeeded they would advise their families to join them. Friends and relatives would also be told that work was to be found, in say Liverpool or London, and these people would, in turn, bring up others. But the great ports and manufacturing towns were already full with economic asylum seekers from the countryside. As a result of this continuing process large overcrowded slums developed in almost every urban area.

By way of an example, the conditions in Liverpool in the 1840's were almost unbelievable. In the 1840's Dr. Duncan, Liverpool's first Medical Officer, drew attention to the fact that many people lived in 'Courts', which consisted of two rows of houses, placed opposite to each other, with only an intervening space of 9 to 15 feet. Needless to say, fresh air could not circulate in such places. Ash pits and privies were frequently emptied, consequently their contents tended to be spread over the 'Court' in great stinking mounds. So far as sewers were concerned, Duncan did not know of a single Court that was linked to the main system. To understand just how bad things were, one has to appreciate that in the 1840's there were 1,982 of these 'Courts' in Liverpool, containing 10,692 houses, inhabited by 55,534 persons. Needless to say, living under these conditions, annual epidemics of typhus, cholera and other diseases regularly ravaged the working class quarters of this great port. (1)

Yet, almost unbelievably, even these appalling conditions were an improvement on housing and working conditions in the countryside! In the first half of the reign of Queen Victoria those ruling Britain were amassing great wealth, but the village labourer had no stake in the wealth his labours were creating. In fact, all farm workers were being paid at starvation rates. Two pence an hour for a man, one penny for a woman, and just one half penny for a child. There were two days holiday a year, and most of the cottages were just 'picturesque', unsanitary hovels. (2)

Young girls – often from families that were not on the very bottom rung in rural society – also left the countryside in countless thousands, many of whom would go into 'service' in the homes of wealthy urban merchants and manufacturers. Their departure to a new life, many miles from home, was a sad time for the whole family.

Leaving Home, 1888

"A good and modest girl, who is also pretty, leaving her home in a rural village for the first time, to enter domestic service, is in a position to appeal to the sympathy of all well-disposed minds. As she stands at the cottage-door, receiving the farewell caress of her mother, while the honest old grandfather, and the little sister bringing even her doll to say good-bye, look on sorrowfully, perhaps wondering at the change in their family life, the departure of this simple country maid, for whom the carrier's wagon is waiting, seems a touching incident of ordinary human experience." (3)

Such were the conditions in urban Britain in the Victorian era when [Sir] George Williams [1821–1905] took steps that would earn him a place in history generally, and also a page in the ongoing story of rambling. George Williams, founder of the Young Men's Christian Association, was born at Dulverton, Somerset, on October 11th 1821. He went to London in 1841, and eventually became partner in the drapery firm, Hitchcock and Williams. He took an active interest in religion and, on June 6th 1844, twelve young men, all but one being employees of Hitchcock, met at his home and founded the Y.M.C.A. He was knighted in 1894, and died at Torquay on 6th November, 1905. (4)

The purpose of the Association was to unite young men in an endeavour to improve themselves physically, mentally and intellectually. In the United Kingdom in 1923 there were 814 branches with a membership of 118,430, while at this time the U.S.A. had 1435 centres with a membership of 1,011,144. The Young Women's Christian Association was formed in 1855 with similar objects to those of the Men's Association. (5)

The Liverpool Y.M.C.A. Rambling Club – Established 1874. The Liverpool Y.M.C.A. was established on 27th July 1846. Gymnastics, cricket and other outdoor games soon became part of the character-building programme. However, the records reveal that in the year 1874 an organised Rambling Club had been established. Among the places they visited in the early years were Knowsley, Hale, Bidston Observatory, Wigan [coal mine visited] and many places on the nearby Wirral peninsular. However, the Asylum at Rainhill and the Kirkdale Gaol clearly stand out as Club favourites in the 1880's.

For the first years of the Club's existence the membership was restricted to young men, but soon girl friends were invited on alternate rambles. Later on pressure clearly built up, character building put at risk, and the 'alternative' was dropped. From then on women were invited to *most* of the rambles, only occasional rambles being reserved exclusively for men. It was, in fact, shortly after one of their regular visits to the Lunatic Asylum that the rules were relaxed even more, when girl friends of members were actually allowed to join the Club!

At some point in the early 1880's Burton village and Burton woods, Wirral, appeared in the Club's programme for the first time. Unfortunately, the village then had the sad distinction of having no pub! Even more unfortunately, in the 1880's it also had no 'refreshment cottage' where tea and scones could be obtained. To rectify this unacceptable state of affairs these pioneer ramblers finally persuaded a farmer's wife to provide modest meals for ramblers at 8d a head! Following this historic break-through such establishments then became very numerous. (6)

From these early years Burton soon became a firm favourite with the Y.M.C.A. Rambling Club. The village also became a firm favourite with ramblers generally, and remains so down to the present day. The photograph on the following page shows members of the Birkenhead Photographic Society [c 1920's] sitting on the verge in front of an old cottage in the centre of the village. The cottage is still standing, the village still has no pub, and all the refreshment shops have closed.

Birkenhead Photographic Society members in Burton village in the 1920's The writer's mother, Mabel Hollett, nee Wise, is fourth from the left on the front row.

The Forest Ramblers' Club – Established 1884. As we have noted, early rambling groups were exclusive, basing their membership on a particular section of late-Victorian society. The London-based 'Sunday Tramps', formed by Leslie Stephen in 1879, drew its male only membership from the literary, political and academic elite of the day, whilst the 'Scottish Cairngorm Club', established in 1887, was firmly based on the professional middle-class.

However, the founding members of the 'Forest Ramblers' were drawn from the retail trade. Set up in 1884, it is still going strong today. The members claim that it is the oldest rambling club in Britain. The name of the club gives an indication of the original aims and objectives of the group, namely to walk through Epping Forest and report the obstructions they encountered. (7)

Unlike the vast majority of walking clubs it was originally, and remains to this day, a mid-week rambling club. The obvious reason for this is that being based on the retail trade its founders were taking advantage of the early closing days. An unusual, dated, feature of the club today is that it still remains a 'male-only' organisation, although special 'Ladies Days' featured on the club agenda from the outset. A typical notice for such an event featured in the club journal for 1886.

FOREST RAMBLERS' CLUB.
LADIES' DAY, WEDNESDAY, JUNE 30th 1886

A Meeting will take place on the above date for a short ramble in the Forest, assemble at Bishopsgate Station, G.E.R. at 2.30. The Club will avail itself of the accommodation provided by the "Finsbury Philanthropic Society." I enclose a couple of tickets with particulars, should you not desire to keep them, kindly do me the favour to return same on or before Monday night.

Jas. H. Porter. Hon. Sec. (8)

Other desirable destinations for London-based rambling groups of the period were listed in 'The Gipsy Journal and British Tourist' Among the places recommended by the editor was Theobalds Park, Holyrood Park, Farnborough and Hampstead Heath. (9) However, Kent, during the Hop Picking season, was not considered to be a suitable area for genteel rambling groups, due to the fact that they would have found it hard to avoid contact with the London under-class. Namely, the Cockney hop-pickers who, among other things, were invariably drunk! Writing in 1886, a reporter for the London press outlined the dreadful state of affairs.

Most of the labourers, he stated, came from the slums of London. Some made their way down in caravans, who were known as the 'Carriage Folk'. These, we are assured, were arrant poachers

90

and thieves. Next were those who came down by train, who were not infrequently seen at stations in a state of drunkenness and, finally, there were the poorest of the poor, who walked down. Concerning those who came down by train and on foot he wrote:

"Some of the Railway travellers are by no means prepossessing fellow-passengers. The other day when travelling I had as a fellow-traveller a young lady, apparently returning from a tennis party, with some friends. I fell into a doze, and on opening my eyes again found that a very ruffianly company had taken her place, a most horrible metamorphosis".

"Finally there are those who walk down. These start weeks before the hopping time, and are a regular curse; some try to pick up a copper by begging, some by singing; there is one point in common, however, (with very few exceptions) with regards to these pedestrians, the women have to carry the household goods (contained in one sack), and do the singing as well, all chivalrous ideas among the men of doing for the gentler (?) sex having disappeared, supposing that they ever existed." (10)

With the Hop Pickers in Kent, 1886 (10)

The Yorkshire Ramblers' Club – Established 1892.
Socially, the famous Yorkshire Ramblers' Club was more or less on the same level as the Cairngorm Club, for it too was supported by the professional middle-classes and, in addition, well-heeled Yorkshire businessmen, or their sons. The preliminary steps to establish this group were taken on 13th July 1892, when Messrs George Lowe, J.A. Green, H.H. Bellinghouse and Herbert Slater met at the house of the last named to discuss the best way of going forward. After an exchange of views it was agreed to call a meeting of 'pedestrians' at the end of the season, Green being nominated to invite those known to be interested in the matter.

The meeting was held in Headingly on 6th October, at which it was unanimously resolved to form a club, and the terms of the resolutions that followed stated its objects. These were, primarily, to organise walking and mountaineering expeditions, "and to encourage in connection therewith the study of nature". The title of the club was then chosen. (11)

Yorkshire Ramblers' Club Territory, North Yorkshire, sketched in 1885

During the first year the constitution of the club took shape, and the question of "qualification" for membership received much attention. The tendency here being to "ever raise the standard." The criteria was that candidates had to be physically fit enough to stand a chance of surviving the club's challenging and varied programme. They were also expected to have an interest in the objects of the Club, which were outlined per Rule Two of the constitution: "To organise walking and mountaineering excursions, and to gather and promote knowledge concerning Natural History, Archaeology, Folk Lore and Kindred Subjects". (12)

In addition to this members were also required to show a keen interest in pot-holing and, as time went on, to have sufficient funds and leisure time to be able to join the many overseas mountaineering expeditions organised by the club. In short the Yorkshire Ramblers' Club was, in practice, more of an 'Outdoor Adventure Club' rather than a group brought together merely in order to ramble. The Club, however, has a long and very distinguished history.

Early in the history of this old-established Club a very important step was taken, namely, to invite certain members of the Alpine Club, and others, to join as honorary members. And, it is interesting to note, the first honorary member to be elected under this ruling was none other than the aforementioned great mountaineer, Edward Whymper who, in 1893, gave a lecture to the club on rock climbing and snowcraft. Exhibitions of mountaineering equipment were subsequently organised, and over the next few years ever-increasing numbers of club members went on long, expensive expeditions, particularly to Switzerland and Norway, where they acquitted themselves well.

All of which, among other things, clearly confirms that apart from being physically fit, as a general rule at least the majority of members must have been drawn from the ranks of the relatively affluent middle-classes. From which, one can reasonably assume, that if some of them were not actually from local land-owning families, they would almost certainly have had a certain degree of empathy with those who did own land, which was invariably crossed by footpaths, a factor that could explain the decidedly non-confrontational line of the Yorkshire Ramblers' Club on footpath preservation issues. All of which surfaced in 1895, just three years after the establishment of the Club:

"Before leaving the question of the transactions of the Club, as touching its meetings, it is as well to mention that originally one of the objects of the club was to actively support the Commons Preservation Society. There has, nevertheless, always been reluctance on the part of the membership to take part in controversies of any kind, and any proceedings which might have led to litigation would have been extremely distasteful to them and quite foreign to the nature of the club. While placing on record their appreciation of the objects of the Commons Preservation Society, and hope that its good work may prosper, a resolution was passed at a special meeting in 1895 that the club should no longer, as a body, bind itself to assist the society, and the rules were altered accordingly". (13)

However, soon after this the Club established strong links with other 'Outdoor Pursuits Groups', a notable one being the Kyndwr Club – a group that had devoted much time and energy to the exploration of the Derbyshire caves. Members of the Yorkshire Club then had an opportunity of hearing about the work of the Kyndwr group in some detail, through a lecture delivered to them by the aforementioned Dr. E.A. Baker, the noted campaigner for Open Access to Mountains in Scotland. (14)

The Yorkshire Ramblers' Club also developed strong links with the Manchester-based Rucksack Club, established their famous library and then, in 1910, began to subscribe to and stock what they termed "Kindred Journals", and among which feature many of the publications produced by the best known mountaineering groups. (15) In addition to all this the Club members, Bullard and Calvert, produced a club song, which captured the flavour of the group and the period. It was presented to club members by J.H. Buckley, at the club's annual dinner in November, 1910. The first two verses are particularly memorable:

There are Clubs diverse and many in the Empires mighty bounds,
But few – if there be any – where such harmony abounds
As in the Yorkshire Ramblers – pot-holers, cragsmen, scramblers –
For we're all the best of fellows in the Yorkshire Ramblers' Club.

Chorus –

The Yorkshire Ramblers: pot-holers, cragsmen, scramblers –
For we're all the best of fellows in the Yorkshire Ramblers' Club.

To see the Ramblers climbing is really quite a treat,
For it sets beholders thinking they have suckers in their feet:
But they haven't it's their muscle and their thews that win the tussle,
Making vertical progression like a walk along the street.   (16)

But war was looming on the horizon, and in a few short years the cragsmen and scramblers of the Yorkshire Ramblers' Club would be facing dangers of an altogether different nature. Out of their comparatively small membership fifty-five served in the in the armed forces during the Great War and, of these, five were killed in action and seven wounded – three of them severely. Another remarkable fact was the number who served either as non-commissioned or commissioned officers, for out of the fifty-five two served as Corporals, four as Sergeants, eighteen as 2nd Lieutenants, two as Lieutenants, six as Captains, four as Majors, two as Lieutenant Commanders and three as Lieutenant Colonels. (17)

Typical of those who fell was Captain Arthur Morris Slingsby, one-time leading light of the Club. Brilliant though his military career had been, the especial interest of the club was centred upon his magnificent mountaineering in the Himalaya. Among many noted exploits, in 1909 he joined with Dr. T.G. Longstaff and Dr. Neve in exploring the then unknown maze of the Eastern Karakoram. They crossed the main range in June by the Saltoro Pass (18,200ft.), and discovered the immense Siachen Glacier, 48 miles long, and to their astonishment piercing the main range, and a feeder of the Indus basin. His obituary, part of which I quote below, serves as a tribute to Slingsby, his Club, and his colleagues, who died so tragically, under similar circumstances, in the 1st Would War:

ARTHUR MORRIS SLINGSBY
1885-1916
"Morris fell on 8tyh March, 1916, in the final battle for the relief of Kut-el-Amara "while most gallantly leading the final rush of the 56th Rifles. On this occasion, as usual, he had worked his way to the head of the attack, and was leading on his men, although as Adjutant his place might well have been in the rear. Still the men trusted him and he knew they would follow him."   (18)

CHAPTER EIGHT
THE SHEFFIELD CLARION RAMBLERS

In 1900 one of the most remarkable of all the early rambling clubs was established. It was the Sheffield Clarion Ramblers, a radical left-wing club which was described by G.B.H. Ward, its founder, and leading-light for many years, as the first Sunday workers' rambling club in the North of England. It all began in the autumn of 1900 when Ward decided to organise a ramble round Kinder Scout. He placed an advertisement in the *Clarion*, a socialist weekly, edited by Robert Blatchford, inviting others to join him. The response was good, and on the first Sunday in September 1900 – which by chance was fine and clear – Ward set out with his small, pioneering entourage of 11 men and 3 women.

On the walk it was agreed that Ward should formally organise some more rambles during 1901, which resulted in five more walks taking place in that year. It was on these walks that the participants decided that the group should be given an official existence. (1) A committee was set up and the group was then formally identified with the socialist cause by being named after Blatchford's famous paper. Robert Blatchford was to have an ongoing influence on socialism and the rambling movement, making a brief glance at his life and times appropriate.

Robert Glanville Blatchford (1851–1943) journalist, author and socialist, was born at Maidstone on the 17th March 1851. Unfortunately, for a future socialist, his poverty stricken, but well-meaning Tory parents decided to name him after the Conservative statesman who had died the previous year! Robert was the second son of an unsuccessful strolling player named John Glanville Blatchford, married to an equally unsuccessful small-part actress, of half-Italian blood, Georgiana Louisa Corri. John Blatchfords's opinions, insofar as he had any, were those of a strong churchman and vehement Conservative. [Although precisely what it was he had to 'Conserve' is not abundantly clear!]

However, John died when Robert was two years old, long before he had the chance to influence him politically, or otherwise. After his father's death Georgiana continued acting for a further eight years in order to provide for Robert and his brother, but she hated the stage, and to keep her sons off it she wisely had them both apprenticed to trades.

When Robert was fourteen he was indentured for seven years to a brush-maker, but when he was twenty he ran away. From this point on he had a varied career, which included enlisting in the 103rd Regiment, and serving as a timekeeper at Northwich for the Weaver Navigation Company. Finally, he turned to journalism, and with great success. In turn he served on the *Sporting Chronicle,* owned by the father of Sir Edward Hulton, *Bell's life in London,* and when Hulton started the *Sunday Chronicle,* in Manchester, in 1885, Blatchford wrote its leaders from London.

Then, in 1887, Blatchford moved from London to Manchester and began to write about the land issue, and the notorious Manchester slums. His experiences made him a socialist, and in 1891 his socialism cost him his exceptionally well-paid post on the *Sunday Chronicle,* where he was then earning £1,000 a year.

Blatchford responded to this challenge by establishing the *Clarion* as a socialist weekly. This he did with his brother Montague, and another Hulton journalist, Edward Francis Fay. For years its circulation remained at about 34,000 copies, but then a series of articles by Blatchford was reprinted as a book called *Merry England,* which eventually sold over two million copies. This major success soon sent the *Clarion* circulation up to 60,000. His socialism, however, was that of William Morris, the poet and socialist; he appeared to know little of Karl Marx and little more, perhaps, of Sidney and Beatrice Webb. Blatchford, however, was never happy with the leaders of the then dominant *Independent Labour Party.* On the outbreak of the South African War this division became sharper, because the Party became pro-Boer, while Blatchford became pro-war. (2)

Nevertheless, Blatchford's brand of socialism and his writings influenced millions, and among them was Lewis Silkin (1889–1972) the solicitor, Labour politician and Government Minister who, like so many of his contemporaries, absorbed a socialist philosophy after reading *Merry England.* And although city born, Silkin was to acquire a passionate love of the English countryside, and then play a leading role in the rambling and outdoor movement. Silkin subsequently translated his love of the countryside into advancing the National Parks and Access to the Countryside Act of 1949. (3) Which, of course, means that ramblers and the general public today owe a great deal to Blatchford for providing the initial ideological motivation which set Silkin on this historic course of action.

Another interesting point that ramblers today should also bear in mind when evaluating Blatchford and the *Clarion* was that in the early decades of the 20th Century there were numerous *Clarion Cafes* and *Clarion Clubs* linked with this socialist paper. And it was at *The Manchester Clarion Café,* in November 1919, that a meeting was held which resulted in the establishment of the Manchester Ramblers' Federation. (4)

Blatchford and his paper the *Clarion* also have another remarkable claim to fame in the annals of British political and industrial history. In the first decade of the 20th Century there was a long and bitter industrial dispute at the vast Bethesda Slate Quarry in North Wales owned by Lord Penrhyn who, at this time, also owned 46,272 acres of land in North Wales. With an estate rent-roll estimated at £67,000, the Penrhyn Quarry, during brisk times, was said to yield a further £150,000 a year. Zealous in the fight to retain the Landowners hallowed place in society, Penrhyn was also one of the principal founders of the North Wales Property Defence Association.

Accordingly and, no doubt, with commendable objectivity, it was through this organisation that Penrhyn placed much evidence before Carrington's Welsh Land Commission, arguing that out of the agricultural part of his estate he had received no income in excess of expenditure for many years! (5)

Unfortunately, during the long and bitter dispute at the Bethesda Quarry, some men were tempted to break ranks and return to work, to which development a Mr W.J. Parry responded by publishing articles in the *Clarion* which Penrhyn considered libellous. They appeared in the paper on 22nd June and the 13th July 1901.

The first one contained the following hard-hitting paragraph:

"We must not lower our standards. It must be a fight to the death with this tyrant. He will stop at nothing to gain his end. He has brought down the traitor's price from thirty pieces of silver to twenty. He gave to each of the men who returned to work a golden sovereign! Who but Lord Penrhyn would have done this? His friends say he is a good sportsman; but evidently he can hit below the belt."

The second alleged libel, however, was more serious, for here Parry, who was fighting a worthy cause, lost the case by quite needlessly going "over-the-top". Clearly manipulating local 'Infant Mortality Returns' by relating them too directly to the dispute, but not accurately enough date-wise, Parry went on to suggest – *in writing* – that Lord Penrhyn was actually glad that the death rate had increased! Predictably, Penrhyn brought an action for libel against Parry, which he won, and received £500 damages and costs. (6)

The Penrhyn slate quarry, Bethesda, 1892

However, to return to Ward and the early days of the Sheffield Clarion Ramblers. Firstly, it has to be understood that in the closing decades of the 19th and the opening decades of the 20th Centuries religious intolerance was very much the order of the day. It was a time when puritanical zealots preached that working people were duty-bound to attend church three times a day, or face endless punishment in the after-life. Yet this was the only completely free day they had in which to enjoy the companionship of fellow ramblers in the open countryside.

Ironically, Ward himself was a Sunday school teacher, but this phase of his existence ended abruptly in 1897 when he was turned out of his local church by his fire-and-brimstone, fundamentalist vicar. This, however, enabled Ward to state, tongue-in-cheek, that the church had actually played an active role in helping to establish the first working-class rambling club in his area. On which point, it is interesting to note, the famous T.A. Leonard, an active church minister, found himself up against similar religious intolerance when he formed the Co-operative Holiday Association in 1891.

Consistent with the Group's ideological foundations, in 1902 local Labour Councillor, Tom Shaw, became the first President of the Sheffield Clarion Ramblers. This post was held for just one year. Shaw was followed by Messrs Kettle, Thickett, Whitney and Venables, until 1909, when the group's founder, G.B.H. Ward was honoured by being asked to serve as president. (7) Ward and his colleagues, now preaching the gospel of rambling, then produced rules [commandments?] the tone of which, in many cases, seemed to be remarkably akin to stern character-building advice preached in the church Ward had left!

"The leader will take the ramble as printed – *wet or fine.* He has charge of the arrangements and will make provision for tea etc., but cannot be responsible for a large party. He should provide a reading or give useful information (place names, etc.) from the S.C.R. booklets or other sources. New members should not defile moor or field with paper or orange peel or leave gates open." (8)

In practice, however, the annual S.C.R. booklets invariably contained so much culturally uplifting material as for example, extracts from the poems of Wordsworth, Coleridge, and other notables, that leaders would hardly, if ever, have needed to refer to any "other sources" when providing their obligatory 'reading.' In addition to this, their walks programmes appear to have been compiled by a puritanical leadership, anxious to purge souls in this life rather than the next one, through participating in exceptionally long, arduous walks! Thus we find, that on the 4th April 1948, G.H. Powell was leading a decidedly challenging 21 mile walk, based on Crook Hill, and C. Booth was leading a walk of 18 miles near Totley Moss on 18th April 1948 (9)

More importantly, however, this group was always to the fore, in the long, ongoing campaign for access to mountain and moorland; their input on the celebrated Kinder Scout Mass Trespass of 1932 being particularly commendable. And among the many poems they published in their famous 'Handbooks' was one by G.B.H. Ward himself, which captures the soul and spirit of this pioneering group. A group that was based on a great Northern, industrial city, surrounded by wild moorland, that was, invariably, 'off limits' to all but the wealthy 'Hunting and Shooting' fraternity.

THE TRESPASSER'S SONG

(Tune: "The Lincolnshire Poacher." Repeat first four bars.)

I am a Clarion Rambler, I wander anywhere;
I go straight up the steepest hill, without a worry or care
I put my pack upon my back, a big heart in my breast;
And when I'm climbing up the hill I seldom take a rest.

CHORUS: Oh 'tis our delight, be it storm or bright, to wander
anywhere.

I am not afraid of sunshine, the rain I never fear;

If I am baked, or if I'm drench'd, I never shed a tear;
I daily wander on my way, no wine is like a spring;
My feast's a crust of bread and cheese, and this grace do I sing –

Oh, 'tis our delight, be it storm or bright, to wander anywhere.

There is no keeper in the Peak whom I could not lose,
And if he watch'd me for a week, I'd tread the moor I chose

That soon the moorlands will be free – my friend a shepherd be –
And then, when we meet on the hill, we'll sing these words with
    glee –

Oh, 'tis our delight, be it storm or bright, to wander anywhere.

To be a Clarion Rambler, and learn to be a man,
And never be a "Flapper" girl, but wander while you can,
Take freedom's way for one and all, proclaim that glorious day;
Lead the proud race of ramblers on, and sing this merry lay –

Oh, 'tis our delight, be it storm or bright, to wander anywhere

And when you get to Peter's gate, and want to go inside,
And wonder what is on your slate – and what there is beside –
You'll only have to nod and say, "Sure you know Father John" (1)
And Peter then will answer you – "Here trespass boards are gone,

For 'tis our delight, be it storm or bright, to wander anywhere.

G.B.H. WARD (1922)

(1)   Father John is our honorary chaplain. He kindly provides the
       weather. But sometimes, when he isn't here, "there's a bit o'
       the divvie in it."

CHAPTER NINE   LONG DISTANCE WALKING

At this point in the history of rambling, walking or 'travelling' it would be appropriate to make a passing mention of our kindred spirits, the individual, competitive or group long distance walkers. The art of long distance walking did not, of course, pass away with the demise of the early travellers, such as Defoe, Goldsmith and Johnson. In fact, there is a long, historical period of over-lap with these famous 'Travellers' and the establishment of athletic and highly competitive walkers. This being particularly so if we take into account Wordsworth and the early and late'Lakers'.

The pioneering days of 'pedestrianism,' in fact, lay between the years 1790 and 1820 when highly competitive walkers were burning up the shoe leather on the highways, bridleways and footpaths of our green and pleasant land. And many of these hardened troopers were intent on establishing records. Foremost among the exponents of this physically demanding new leisure pursuit was an appropriately 'umble but exceptionally energetic lawyer's clerk – Foster Powell.

Foster Powell.   Foster Powell was born in Horsfall, Yorkshire, in 1734. A fast walker, but a slow starter, he was already thirty years old when he set out on his first high-speed, long-distance trek. This was a 50 mile endurance test along the Bath Road. Inappropriately clad in a heavy greatcoat and leather breaches he covered the entire 'walk' in just seven hours!

Not content with this, in 1773 he set out on a decidedly more impressive endurance test. This was a 402 mile 'ramble' from London to York and back, which he undertook to complete in six days, but actually finished in six hours under the stipulated time! Foster Powell's next astonishing feat was to walk the 112 miles from Canterbury to London Bridge and back in 24 hours, and this "he accomplished to the astonishment of some thousands of spectators who were awaiting with anxious desires for his safe arrival". Famous throughout Britain, he subsequently set out to improve on his time for the Canterbury walk, but lost his way. Unfortunately, the shame of this failure crushed him, to the extent that he died a bitterly disappointed man on 15th April 1793. (1)

Robert Barclay Allerdice – "Captain Barclay." Without a doubt, it must be emphasised, one of the greatest walkers who ever lived was the Scotsman, Robert Barclay Allardice, who was more widely known as 'Captain Barclay'. One of his greatest feats took place on 1st June 1809 when he matched himself to set out on a 1,000 mile ramble in a 1,000 successive hours, at the rate of one mile in each and every hour. Or put another way, he set out to walk 1,000 miles in just over 41 days, this being at the rate of 24 miles every day. This he accomplished, and though in the later days he seemed to struggle, he finished well, for he did the last mile in 22 minutes.

"On another occasion Barclay started at 5 am one August morning from the house of Colonel Murray Farquharson, of Allanmore, in Aberdeenshire, to shoot grouse on the mountains, travelling at least thirty miles. By five in the afternoon he returned to dinner, and in the evening set off for his own house at Ury, sixty miles off, and walked the distance in eleven hours without once stopping to refresh. He attended to his ordinary business at home, and in the afternoon walked to Laurencekirk, sixteen miles, where he danced at a ball during the night and returned to Ury by seven in the morning. He did not retire to bed, but occupied the day in partridge shooting in the fields of his own estate. Thus he travelled not less than 130 miles, supposing he only walked eight miles in the course of the day's shooting at home, and also danced at Laurencekirk, without sleeping for two nights and nearly three days." (2)

Joseph Edge, old Mr. Eustace and "Molly." Also ranking high on the list of decidedly fit long-distance walkers is Joseph Edge of Maclesfield. In 1806, when sixty two years of age, he walked 172 miles in 49 hours and twenty minutes; and a Mr Eustace who, at the age of seventy-seven, walked from Liverpool to London in four days. Nor was it men alone who could walk such incredible distances. When long distances had to be covered, and fares on coaches or wagons were such that they prevented working people using them, many women also undertook journeys on foot that would astound our present generation.

One of the most amazing of these was an energetic, early 19th century Lake-land soul known simply as 'Molly.' One memorable day she set out on a tramp from London to her home-town of Keswick, carrying with her a small table! Rather surprisingly, she accomplished her unenviable task, although later she did concede to a friend that "I's niver sa tired of anything in my life as o'that teable". (3)

William Gale, and the great walk at Brompton. The great pedestrian competition in which William Gale, of Cardiff, was engaged at the Lillie Bridge Grounds, West Brompton, in the late summer and autumn of 1877, attracted much public attention. Under the rules of the competition William Gale and his fellow competitors, were obliged to walk each mile and a half at the commencement of each hour. Consequently, on Sunday 26th August 1877, William Gale started to walk 1,500 miles in 1,000 hours, one mile and a half to be walked regularly at the commencement of each hour. This meant that he was bound to walk for six weeks at the rate of thirty-six miles every day. Writing about this on 6th October, the day the great race finished, a member of the London press commented:

"William Gale has already accomplished many great feats in walking. Among other achievements, he has covered 1,000 quarters of a mile in consecutive intervals of ten minutes, thus walking a mile and a half per hour for a fortnight, during the whole of which time he never rested for more than seven minutes at a time. His average pace is about four miles per hour; but his thousandth mile, which was accomplished last Saturday week, only occupied ten minutes. He generally starts rather stiffly, but this soon wears off; and he is in apparent health and sanguine of success. His present performance should be finished this day (Saturday October 6th), at five o'clock in the afternoon." (4)

William Gale walking 1,500 miles in a thousand hours

W. Corkey and 'Blower' Brown. The great six-day walking contest held at the Agricultural Hall, Westminster, terminated on the first Saturday in November, 1878. The finish was watched by an audience of 20,000 people. Writing about this on the

9th of the month a reporter for the London press drew attention to the fact that accidents had happened to Vaughan, Crossland, and Weston, which had forced them to withdraw. (The unfortunate Weston, as we shall see was, in fact, one of the most remarkable 'pedestrians' who ever lived.)

These unlucky incidents left the end result firmly in the hands of the two remaining 'favourites' W. Corkey and 'Blower' Brown. For hour after hour – indeed day after day – these two stalwarts stuck close together pounding the track. But gradually the gap between Corkey and 'Blower' widened, so that shortly after 7 p.m. on the Saturday evening Corkey had covered 520 miles which left his worthy rival about 19 miles behind. A table of the distance accomplished by the eighteen who stuck the course to the bitter end, shows that Corkey covered 521 miles, 'Blower' 506, down to the last two Messrs Barnett, 255 miles, and Smythe, 223 miles. The illustration below shows the scene at the end of the contest, with the valiant Corkey heading for victory in front of competing pedestrians on the course.

Finish of the Great Walking-Match, Islington, November 1878 (5)

Weston's Temperance Walk of 5,000 miles in 100 days.
Early in 1884, Weston, the great American Temperance leader and
'Pedestrian', set himself the modest task of promoting his worthy
cause by walking 5,000 miles in 100 days! Early in March, close to
the final stage of this bone-crushing, super-marathon, the *Daily
Telegraph* reported on one of the final stages of this altogether
amazing event – the long, non-stop-trek from Brighton, on the south
coast, to London:

"Weston started out of Brighton on his ninety-fourth stage at
three o'clock a.m. Although he had had only about a couple of
hours sleep he appeared wonderfully fresh, at once got into a capital
gait, and passed through Preston at 3.40. From thence over Clayton
Hill and by Hassock's Gate, he arrived at St. John's Common just as
day was breaking. Soon after seven o'clock he reached Cuckfield
(fourteen miles), and there halted at the road to partake of some
refreshments, which had been prepared for him by the Rev. F.J.
Mount. Although pressed to do so, however, Weston would not
enter the Vicarage, having previously announced his intention of
covering the whole journey without a break.

"At the same steady pace he completed twenty-three and a
half miles at Crawley by 9.40. Up to that time very few people had
been met on the road, here a large number of spectators had
assembled, and along the rest of the route crowds were waiting in
every village. At noon Reigate was just skirted, the American
bearing off to the right along the Merstham Road. About four miles
from Croydon some mounted policemen rode up, and on reaching
the town a body of constables formed on either side, and escorted
the pedestrian through an immense concourse of people on foot, on
horseback, and in vehicles. A heavy shower of rain thinned the
crowd somewhat between Croydon and Streatham, but, before the
latter was reached, the crowd was greater than ever.

"At Kennington Park the throng received fresh additions from the visitors that had lately witnessed the football match at the Oval, but the police managed admirably, and the pedestrian, by way of Kennington Road and Oakley Street, arrived at the Victoria Coffee Place a few minutes before six o'clock. He had thus covered a distance of fifty-three miles on the road without a rest – a marvellous effort, considering the exertions he has undergone. As he entered the building he was enthusiastically cheered." (6)

Weston's Temperance Walk of 5,000 miles in 100 days – his arrival at the Victoria Coffee Hall, Waterloo Road

The Thousand Mile Walk of a Vegetarian. In May, 1903 a fascinating report appeared in *Manchester Guardian* which advised readers that some five years previously a Mr. George Allen, then age thirty six, had decided to give up a meat diet and live simply on vegetables. A keen athlete, Mr. Allen was, apparently, a member of the Finchley Harriers. Living chiefly on meat he had done well for his club, but living on vegetables he claimed that he was in better form than ever! To prove the value of his meat-free diet Allen undertook to walk a thousand miles in twenty days. "This is a serious task and so Mr. Allen regards it." The reporter then continued:

"The fifty miles a day of his itinerary he has accomplished pretty easily up to now, and he has some hours yet in hand. He started from Glasgow on Monday, when Mr. W. Harrison, of Manchester, and members of the Vegetarian Society, wished him good speed. He walked to Beattock on the first day, a distance of 56.5 miles. On the second day he got to Penrith, which carried him to a distance of 113 miles. On Wednesday Lancaster was reached, and so 160.5 miles had been covered. Manchester was the next stopping place, and the Cobden statue in St. Anne's Square was the location."

Within a short space of time news of Allen's arrival spread like wildfire through the city. Without hesitation, vegetarians eating at the many 'Vegetarian Cafes', then thriving in Central Manchester, abandoned their culinary delights, and rushed off to welcome the Champion of their cause. After a short rest and a Turkish bath Allen had a conversation with a representative of the *Manchester Guardian*. From this it would appear that Allen had lived for some time at a "Vegetarian Colony" at Stroud in Gloucester, where the members had sought to establish whether they could live on a meat free diet. "It all worked well," said Mr Allen, "and I am a stronger man than when I lived on beef. I now live simply on garden produce." After giving details of his diet to

113

the press he set off once more, bound for Southport via Rochdale, where it was his intention to rest on the Sunday, before heading south for London, which he was scheduled to reach on 16th July. (7)

The Manchester to Southport Walk of 1903. Another great walking event also took place in May 1903, this was the celebrated 'Manchester to Southport Walk.' The route of the walk was discussed by a Planning Committee, which met on 12th May. Significantly, the route finally presented was one that avoided Wigan, primarily, because the cobbled lanes on the Southport side of the town would, it was felt, have been difficult to walk on at high speed. The elders of the committee were, however, at pains to point out that they had no particular prejudice against the town! The best interests of the walkers, the residents of Wigan were earnestly assured, was the *only* factor in their minds when reaching this far-reaching decision.

After outlining the said route in remarkable detail, the report concluded by stating that the committee had had several applications from men who wished to walk for a wager. However, it is pleasing to record, all applications of this dubious nature had been refused. There was, the public were assured, to be no reward for competitors except the bronze medals which were to be presented to all who managed to finish the forty one miles in ten hours. The Mayor of Southport had agreed to preside at the Celebration Dinner, to be held at the Prince of Wales Hotel. Several manufacturers of patent foods, it is interesting to note, had agreed to send motor-cars stocked with foods suitable for the competitors.

The great walk itself took place on Saturday 23 May. The reporter for *The Guardian* described the event as "a most strenuous piece of athleticism". Two men completed the journey at the astonishing rate of five and four-fifths of a mile per hour. A hundred reached Southport within ten hours of the start, and two young Manchester women, who finished the course, proved that long-distance walking, at a good pace, is by no means a sport exclusively for "mere men."

At the conclusion of the race there was an official dinner at the Prince of Wales Hotel at which the Mayor of Southport presented the winner – a dental technician by the name of Ormerod – with a valuable silver cup and a photograph showing the scene at the finish. The great race, however, had been a close run event, for Ormerod had completed the course in 7 hours, 11 minutes and 8 seconds, whilst the runner-up, a Mr John E Rankin took just two seconds longer. (8)

Three more amazing records. The enthusiasm for long-distance, "high-speed" walking continued. For example, in 1904 a Dr. A.W. Wakefield set out from Keswick and made the round of eleven peaks in 19 hours and 53 seconds. The following year he eclipsed this walk by climbing Robinson and 18 other peaks, and being back again in Keswick in 22 hours and 7 minutes. He had ascended 23,500 feet, and walked a distance of 22 miles. The sport spread to North Wales where, in 1938, a local sheep-farmer, Mr. T. J. Firbank, walked over 14 peaks, totalling an incredible 52,000 feet, in 8 hours and 25 seconds. Not to be outdone, however, his equally fit wife then made the same circuit in just 9 hours and 29 minutes, (9)

The Long Distance Walkers' Association: A Brief History. After the 2nd World War, during the 1950's and early 1960's, the activity of long-distance walking received a boost from the late Dr. Barbara Moore, whose epic trips up and down the United Kingdom, and across America, made headline news. "Following on from these achievements others became involved in creating challenge walks – some in keeping with the feats of Dr. Moore's, but others aimed at the perhaps less physically capable individuals. The 'Billy Butlin' ultimate Land's End to John O'Groats walk in 1960 attracted 3,000 entries, and the annual *Kent*

Messenger organised event for the 50 mile route from Margate to Maidstone sometimes exceeded 10,000 starters. In those early days, the majority of such events were held on roads but gradually, and no doubt in part influenced by the creation of the Pennine Way National Trail, an interest developed in traffic free rural type long-distance walks."

"The popularity of challenge walks both from a participating and organisational point of view increased to the extent that by the early 70's, there were in excess of twenty events available. These extending from seventeen to fifty miles in length held throughout England with others coming to notice in Wales, Ireland and the Netherlands. In addition, other long-distance footpaths were being created to supplement the Pennine Way. The need to service this interest was recognised by a number of individuals and in 1971, Alan Blatchford, and his walking colleague, Chris Steer, decided to take action. The Long Distance Walkers Association (LDWA) was created." (10) Brian Smith, of the LDWA, continues the story of the Association:

"Advertisements were placed in various outdoor journals and, in early 1972, copies of the first LDWA newsletter were sent out free to 200 potential members but with advice that unless a minimum 35p subscription was paid, no further copies would be delivered! Chris was the person with the practical knowledge, he having already organised several challenge events, including the Tanners Marathon which is still being held to this day".

"The Association has developed over the years from the purely Challenge Walk interest group which originally brought it into being. The single aim of the LDWA is to further the interests of those who enjoy long distance walking. In endeavouring to achieve that aim, the Association gained recognition as the Sports Council Governing Body for the activity of long distance walking. And while that status is probably not as valuable as when it was

116

achieved in 1985, it has allowed the Association to take an active part in making representation in all manner of relevant topics. This includes recognition by such as the Countryside Commission, Scottish Natural Heritage and the Countryside Council for Wales."

"Since 1995, the President of the Association has been Sir John Johnson a former Chairman of the Countryside Commission. He is a keen walker who has climbed all the Munros and completed many of the long distance routes." As at December 2000 membership was approximately 7,000. The vast majority are residents of the U.K. but there is representation in mainland Europe, Australia and America. (11)

CHAPTER TEN
THE LAKE DISTRICT AND THE 'LAKERS'

No work on rambling would be complete without making reference to the Lake District and the 'Lakers' and, in particular, Wordsworth. The area is enormously popular, to the extent that long before the arrival of the railways and working-class ramblers, wealthy upper and middle-class people were making the long trek north to the English Lake District. In the early days most arrived as tourists, but a proportion of them soon decided to take up residence in the area and, in many cases, by building great mansions on the banks of Windermere.

It was, of course, Wordsworth, together with Coleridge, Southey, De Quincey, Martineau and Ruskin who led the 19th Century literary and artistic elite that soon became known as the 'Lakers' or 'Lakists.' Collectively, they did much to popularise the area, but before them many other writers, poets and intellectuals had left their mark. Men such as Thomas West, William Hutchinson, Thomas Gray, William Hutton, Joseph Wise, the poet of Holm Cultram Abbey, and William Gilpin, the acknowledged 'High Priest' of the cult of the 'Picturesque,' and many others, had all made their own individual contribution towards the popularisation of the Lakes.

In 1778 Thomas West's well-known *Guide to the Lakes* appeared. (1) This work was to be one of the most popular of all the Guides, ten editions being printed by 1812. (2) In addition to this, between 1780 and 1810 many of the serious artists of the day worked in the Lake District, among whom were Towne, Wheatly, Rowlandson, J.M.W. Turner, William Turner of Oxford and Crome. (3) All of which complemented the work of the Lake writers and poets, which persuaded more and more 'fashionable' people to head for this beautiful, but remote corner of England.

Wordsworth, Coleridge and Southey had much in common; all three wrote poetry, and in their youth were decidedly radical. Nevertheless, as time went by all three found themselves sailing towards the same port, for in their mature years they all became firm adherents of the Church of England and, in their old age they had become unmistakable Tories! (4) As Jacobins, and then as Tories, this famous trio were, after all, primarily well educated middle-class Englishmen who, as the years ticked by, did what many have done before and since – dropped back into, and served as pillars of the establishment, albeit, with regrets and profound reservations.

Nevertheless, it still fell to William Wordsworth to set the tone for the radical 'Rambling Revolution' that was to emerge in full force, within a few short decades of his death in 1850. A keen rambler throughout his long life, he probably knew the mountains, moors, fells and valleys of the Lake District as well as any man who ever lived. Wordsworth was, it should be noted, a mighty rambler, for De Quincy calculated that "he must have traversed a distance of 175,000 to 180,000 English miles – a mode of exertion which, to him, stood in the stead of alcohol and all other stimulants whatever to the animal spirits". (5)

In 1779 he made an excursion through Dovedale to Penrith, and rambled with his sister and her friend, Mary Hutchinson. The following year Wordsworth's really serious rambling began, for in 1790 he resolved to make a foreign tour with his friend, Robert Jones of Plas-yn-Llan, Denbighshire. The two young men set out with £20 each and, according to all accounts, carrying everything they required in pocket handkerchiefs! They left Dover on 13th July 1790 and on arrival in France found the people were 'mad with joy' in the early stages of the revolution, and were welcomed as representatives of British liberty! (6)

In November 1791, Wordsworth left England and made a further tour of France. He returned to England in December 1792, and soon after this Joseph Johnson, a radical publisher, brought out his *Evening Walk* and early in 1793 his *Descriptive Sketches*. Later in the same year Wordsworth went on another long tour, this time across Salisbury Plain, and then Tintern Abbey, in the Wye Valley, to his friend Jones in Wales. (7)

Wordsworth's friendship with Coleridge dates from 1795. The most notable 'Rambler Related' incident of this period being a walk they made together on 13th November 1797, on which the two poets proposed to compose a joint ballad to be sold for £5 to pay for the cost of a proposed tour. The *Ancient Mariner*, thus began, was left to Coleridge to complete. Coleridge, like his great friend, Wordsworth, was also a notable rambler.

During his time at Cambridge Samuel Taylor Coleridge, who was to become the great poet and philosopher, made a notable walking tour with his college friend, Joseph Hucks. Their adventure began in June 1794, when the two set off with the intention of doing most of their walking in Wales, apart from a brief diversion to Oxford to meet up with old friends. Coleridge left Cambridge without a degree, six months after making this tour. Their adventure on this six hundred mile ramble was recorded for posterity by Hucks in a little book entitled *A Pedestrian Tour in Wales,* which was published in 1795. It was, however, before the publication of this work that Coleridge was introduced to Robert Southey at Balliol College, Oxford. In the first decade of the 19th Century the lives of the Wordsworths, Coleridge and Southey began to interrelate more and more.

In 1812 Wordsworth applied to Lord Lonsdale to obtain some sort of situation for him. This soon led to him being offered the position of "Distributor of Stamps" for the county of Westmoreland at £400 a year. A great deal of the real work, however, was undertaken by his clerk, John Carter, who served him all his life, and also edited the *Prelude* after his death. The post was, in fact, formally transferred to Wordsworth's son William, in 1842, who, since 1831, had actually been working with Carter at the Stamp Office.

Upon the death of Southey (21st March 1843) the position of poet-laureate was offered to Wordsworth who at first declined, but then accepted the honour. Sadly, a few short years after this Wordsworth, the one-time left-wing radical was to devote much of his time and effort to opposing the construction of the Kendal and Windermere Railway Line, on the questionable grounds that it would bring undesirable working-class people to the Lake District – people who would clearly be intellectually incapable of appreciating the beauty of the Lake District as, of course, only he and his select band of 'Lakers' could!

Wordsworth's well-known fight against the construction of the Kendal and Windermere Line was, to an appreciable extent, fought out in the pages of the regional and national press. In a long letter to the *Morning Post* of 11th December, 1844, he listed damning 'evidence' that "imperfectly educated" tourists were incapable of appreciating the beauty of the Lakes! For example – "In the midst of a small pleasure ground, immediately below my house rises a detached rock, equally remarkable for the beauty of its form, and the ancient oak that grows out of it." "What a nice place this would be," said a Manchester tradesman pointing to the rock, "if that ugly lump were but out of the way".

From this, and similar horrifying examples of plebeian vulgarity, Wordsworth moved on rapidly. Firstly, he made it clear that in view of this lamentable state of affairs no good at all was to be obtained by transferring large numbers of uneducated people to places such as the Lake District. He was, however, generous enough to concede that the 'lower orders' would benefit, educationally, by being encouraged to walk in the countryside, *provided* such tentative excursions into the 'great-out-doors' were confined to half-day walks in fields near their own large town or city! Wordsworth's feeling on the issue were summed up in the following poem with which he chose to conclude his letter to the *Morning Post*:

> Proud were ye, Mountains, when, in times of old,
> Your Patriot sons, to stem invasive war,
> Intrenched your brows; ye gloried in each scar:
> Now for your shame, a power the Thirst of Gold,
> That rules o'er Britain like a balefull star,
> Wills that your peace, your beauty, shall be sold,
> And clear way made for her triumphal car
> Through the beloved retreats your arms enfold!
> Heard ye that Whistle? As her long-linked Train
> Swept onwards did the vision cross your view?
> Yes, ye were startled; and in balance true,
> Weighed the mischief with the promised gain,
> Mountains, and Vales, and Floods, I call on you
> To share the passion of a just disdain.

Alas, poor Wordsworth lost the fight, and ye mountains were left to face their plight! The formal opening of the line took place at Kendal station on Tuesday 20th April,1847. At 10 am the assembled crowd cheered as "a "Triumphal Car" composed of sixteen carriages, accompanied by a brass band, and laden with a 'full freight' of passengers, pulled out of Kendal station. Just two hours later another train of eighteen carriages, with yet another brass band followed. To celebrate the event there was a grand 'Dejeuner' at the Royal Hotel, Bowness, at 2.30 p.m., followed by a dinner at the Crown Hotel, Bowness at 5 p.m.

It was at the second event that Nicholson, one of the prime movers in this development, decided to respond to the Poet

122

Laureate's sustained attack on the construction of the line, and the coming influx of working people that it would bring to the Lakes. He began by stating that the railway opened that day would especially benefit the operative classes, the large mass of the population residing in the manufacturing districts, who ought to be reckoned as intelligent beings, fully capable of being influenced by the beauties of the Lake District. The press report on the event then went on to note that the poet had not only attacked the railway at great length in the columns of the *Morning Post*, but also in one of his terse and beautiful sonnets. But revenge is sweet – the Cumbrian press then published a 'reply' in the form of a 'Wordsworth style sonnet, written by R.M. Milnes, MP,

"The hour may come, nay must in these our days
When the swift steam-car with the cat'ract's shout
Shall mingle its harsh roll, and motley rout
Of multitudes, these mountain echoes raise
But thou, the Patriarch of these beauteous ways
Canst never grudge that gloomy streets send out,
The crowded sons of labour, care and doubt,
To read these scenes by light of thine own lays,
Disordered laughter and encounter rude
The Poet's finer sense perchance may pain,
But many a glade and nook of solitude,
For quiet walk and thought will still remain,
Where He those poor intruders can elude,
Nor lose one dream for all their homely gain." (8)

Aira Force

The age of steam, and the age of tourism had, indeed, arrived in the Lakes and, in response to this more and more 'Guides' were to be written during the second half of the 19th Century. One of the best of these was *The Complete Guide to the English Lakes,* by the 'Late-Laker' Harriet Martineau. The first edition was published in 1855, in which she gave useful, every-day advise on such matters as the coach fare from Windermere railway station, and information about the Windermere, Ullswater and Coniston steamers. (The first steamer to be launched on Winderemere, was the 49 ton vessel "Lady of the Lake" which entered the water in June, 1845.)

Launch of the "Lady of the Lake" steamer, on Windermere, 1845

However, what really lifts Martineau's *Guide* head and shoulders above the competition is her views on local people. Thankfully, as a realist, she did not see them through the patronising eyes of the 'Picturesque Traveller' Gilpin or, on the other hand, was she burdened with the 'romantic' illusion that here, in the Lake District, the peasantry were, or had been living in some sort of 'ideal' rural paradise. All of which comes across loud and clear when she is writing about the poor, upland Cumbrian 'Statesman,' the small, independent farmers, who owned their own small 'estates' who, in reality, she felt, were merely existing as subsistence level peasants. She wanted them to join the 'real world' (9) In 1870 Martineau's *Biographical Sketches* were published, in which it is also interesting to note her comments about Wordsworth's opposition to the construction of the Windermere Railway:

"It was rather a serious matter to hear the Poet's denunciation of the railway, and to read his well-known sonnets on the desecration of the Lake Region by the unhallowed presence of commonplace strangers; and it was truly painful to observe how his scornful and grudging mood spread among the young, who thought they were agreeing with Wordsworth in claiming the vales and lakes as a natural property for their enlightened selves." (10)

Harriet Martineau

Unfortunately, Martineau's contemporary, the great John Ruskin, was most decidedly *not* in favour of railways – in the Lake District or anywhere else for that matter! Nevertheless, he was 'on the side of the angels' on other issues. A wealthy man, in 1871 Ruskin founded the *St. George's Guild,* the forerunner of our present-day Housing Associations. This involved a cash donation of £7,000 to the new institution, and also a London freehold worth a further £3,500, all of which was placed under the management of the famous Miss Octavia Hill, who was appointed as the first manager. (11)

The life and times of Miss Octavia Hill are, or course, very central to the whole history of the rambling and 'out-of-doors' movement. Firstly, she was a very active member of *The Commons Preservation Society,* and secondly, in conjunction with Canon Rawnsley and Sir Robert Hunter, founded "the National Trust." (12)

Ruskin, like Wordsworth, saw himself as the defender of the Lake District, under threat from a perceived, danger posed by steam power. The protest led by Robert Somervell and John Ruskin, in 1876, against the extension of railways in the Lake District, and his involvement in the establishment of "the Lake District Defence Society" in 1883, are notable. The latter being a move to oppose plans to build the Braithwaite and Buttermere Railway.

The battle on the 1876 issue continued, during which Ruskin made many derogatory remarks about working people. He also issued an invitation to all persons to sign a petition to Parliament to prevent the extension of railways in general running though the Lake District. Predictably, *Punch* decided to deflate Ruskin, by exposing his pompous elitism, which the periodical did brilliantly by publishing a satirical poem, written in his own style, entitled *Lady of the Lake Loquitur.* This was illustrated by a caricature of

Ruskin wielding a large sword, Don Quixote fashion, over the mangled wreck of a steam train! (13)

"Lady of the Lake Loquiter"

However, to return briefly to Wordsworth. At heart, I believe, there was always something of the 'rebel' left in Wordsworth, even in old age, which the following snippet will emphasise. When reporting on a footpath dispute in the Lake District in October, 1887, a reporter opened by recalling that at one time Wordsworth was journeying to Lowther Castle to be present at a dinner given in his honour, in company with Mr. Justice Coleridge and the Lord Chief Justice. They passed down Patterdale by Ullswater, then, leaving the chaise, they struck across some fields towards the castle:

"Suddenly" the report continued "the path ended in a blind wall. The poet muttered something and attacked the fence as if it were a living enemy and, crying out- "This is the way, an ancient right of way too" passed on. That evening after the ladies had left the room Mr Justice Coleridge said to Sir John Wallace, who was a near resident and a guest, "Sir John, I fear we committed trespass today; we came over a broken down wall on your estate." Sir John seemed nettled, and said that he wished he could have caught the man who broke it down; he would horsewhip him. The grave old bard at the end of the table heard the words, the fire flashed in his face, and rising to his feet he answered, "I broke your wall down Sir John. It was obstructing an ancient right of way, and I will do it again. I am a Tory at heart, but scratch me on the back deep enough and you will find the whig in me yet." (14)

Needless to say, the atmosphere at this notable dinner party was somewhat frosty following the Bard's entirely justifiable outburst. An outburst which, nevertheless, drew attention to the whole issue of ancient rights of way and, at this point, quite inadvertently, the value of tourism to the economy of the Lake District. Accordingly, by 1887 many of the more astute Cumbrian landowners were in favour of seeing paths were open, and in good order. Nevertheless, the writer for the *Manchester Guardian* responsible for reporting on this issue in 1887 had to concede that there still remained a minority of landowners in the area who felt quite hostile to tourists and what they termed "Mountain Rangers".

Attention should also be given at this point to the notable fight to save Latrigg Fell for the public in 1887. The owner of the Latrigg Estate, near Keswick, and his agent, had suddenly decided to prevent all access to the summit of Latrigg by erecting barbed wire fences, and planting trees across the line of the path. Thankfully, the prompt response was the establishment of the Keswick and District Footpath Preservation Association.

129

Responding to this development the landowner tried the well-known diversionary tactic of trying to discredit the responsible leadership and members of the Association. This they did by calling the Association a mob of loafers! Among these so-called "Loafers," it is interesting to note, were Ministers of Religion, Doctors, Solicitors, a Member of the House of Commons and, very significantly, quite a few enlightened local Landowners!

The upshot of all this was that on the 6th September 1887 between four and five hundred people assembled at Fawre Park and, on Sunday 1st October about two thousand people walked to the top of Latrigg. The battle for access on this fell continued for some time after this, but as Henry Irwin Jenkinson said, back in October 1887, the people of Keswick who were present on Latrigg Fell on this great, historic day, were fighting the battle for *all* lovers of the Lake District and, instead of being slighted and sneered at as they were, they ought to have had the respect, the thanks and the help of everyone. (15)

The steam vessel *Gondola* on Coniston lake, Lancashire, July 1860

"The *Gondola,* as she is named, now floats on Coniston Water, Lancashire, one of the most charming of our lakes, recently made easily accessible to tourists from the metropolis and the chief towns by the extension of the Furness Railway to within a short distance of the head of the lake." – "The vessel is the property of certain noblemen and gentlemen connected with the Furness Railway. It has been built to convey tourists round the lake, at intervals during the day, and for the use of private pleasure parties at other times. The *Gondola* was designed by Mr. James Ramsden, the secretary and general manager of the Furness Railway: it was built by Messrs Jones and Co. of Liverpool, under the inspection of Mr. Douglas Hebson. Very great credit is due to Mr. Ramsden for the novelty of the design and for the tasteful manner in which the details have been completed. The *Gondola* is commanded by one of the intrepid men who formed the crew of Sir Leopold in the recent voyage of the *Fox* to the Arctic regions." (16)

CHAPTER ELEVEN
SOME EARLY 20th CENTURY RAMBLING CLUBS

The Manchester Rucksack Club.   No serious rambling club existed in the great northern city of Manchester before 1902, the year when the famous Manchester Rucksack Club was established. All of which is rather odd, for by this time the London-based 'Sunday Tramps' had been in existence for twenty-three years and the Yorkshire Rambling Club had, as already noted, been going strong since 1892.   Nevertheless, there   was, at this time in Manchester, a number of local members of the Alpine Club. Many of these were, in fact, of more than regional fame, e.g., Herman Woolley, explorer of the Caucasus Mountains; Charles Pilkington, who first charted the climbs in Skye and Professor Dixon, who had climbed in the Rockies. (1)

Yet the fact still remained that there was no organisation in Manchester, at this time, to band together those who had an interest in rambling, fell-tramping or rock climbing. There were two men, however, A.E. Burns and J.H. Entwistle, who had tramped together in the hill regions of Derbyshire and in the Welsh mountains for many years, and it was these men who were to be instrumental in setting up the Rucksack Club. Firstly, in May 1901, Entwistle read a copy of the Yorkshire Ramblers' Club Journal, in which, he noted, was a record of their Annual Dinner and one passage in a speech of Dr. Collier on that occasion which may be said to be the seed germ of the Club.   This was discussed, the idea slumbered, then was fanned to life again in 1902, when there appeared in the *Manchester City News* an excellent leader entitled *In Praise of Walking Tours* which contained the following summary of the writer's views:

"From the point of view of pure pleasure no one who has once tasted the delights of the pedestrian can decline to more effeminate modes of progression. Ash plant in hand, and in his pocket a pouch of tobacco, and a sufficiency of coin of the realm he has the whole world at his feet. He can go where he likes and stay as long as he likes, independent of trams and trains and petty bonds of civilisation. With all his belongings on his back he is prepared for any contingency – except a continuous downpour of rain. With "the long brown path" before him, and the welcome of an Inn, the sure goal of the day's march, he is equal to any man, and would not change places with millionaire or King." (2)

As a result of this article the editor received, and published in succeeding issues, a batch of appreciative letters, which included one from a man who told readers that he had just completed a delightful 'Walking Tour' with his wife. The route they had taken was from Ripon, Studley, Fountains Abbey, Tanfield, various other places, and then across the moors to Richmond. Their practice, apparently, had been to send their luggage ahead each morning by rail to the place where they intended staying the night. All of which, he assured readers, had proved to be most enjoyable." He concluded, "The cost was less than half of what we should have spent at a popular watering-place, and out of all proportion to the amount of pleasure we derived from the trip". (3)

All this correspondence, of course, made it very evident that, in and around Manchester, there resided a considerable number of people who were very interested in Rambling. Noting all this, the old idea of establishing a club was discussed once more by Burns and Entwistle. The end result of this was that they decided to send their own letter to *The City News*, which was published in September. It began:

"Sir, The general tone of the correspondence which has resulted from your leader on the pleasure of walking tours seems to indicate that this is an opportune moment in which to suggest the formation of a Ramblers' Club for Manchester Pedestrians. That such an institution would greatly enhance the pleasure of tramping and climbing we firmly believe." (4)

Contrary to their expectations, however, the response was not very encouraging. Nevertheless, they finally decided to call a meeting in the County Forum, Manchester, on Monday 13th October 1902, which was presided over by Robert Blackwell. Thirty people were present, but out of these ten did not go much beyond enrolment. The interesting thing about this gathering was the fact that although those present were said to come from 'all stations' in life' for some inexplicable reason a remarkably high proportion of them happened to be lawyers!

All those present, however, were alive to the fact that there was an urgent need to establish a club to serve their interests. Without delay a sub-committee was set up, and a scheme was formulated, which was presented to a second meeting held at the Deansgate Hotel on 24th October 1902. At this the group became a living reality under the title of the Manchester Rucksack Club, which was subsequently changed to the Rucksack Club. The first president was Harold B. Dixon, the first joint secretaries, Messrs Entwistle and Burns. (5)

In practice, their 'rambles' programme was almost, but not quite as challenging as the one devised by the Yorkshire Ramblers' Club, for it included a great deal of scrambling and heavy hill-trekking. Like the Yorkshire Club they also set up their own library and, in 1912, they took a great step forward by opening the first climbing hut in Britain, at Cwm Eigiau, North Wales. The members also raked the country from end to end for 3,000ft peaks to conquer and, having planted their hobnails on all of them, sighed for more worlds to conquer, and started on the 2,500 footers. (6)   As most people are aware, the Rucksack Club never looked back from these early days.

'Trespassers will be prosecuted' (7)

The Manchester Pedestrian Club. Another interesting upshot of the interest roused by the 'In Praise of Walking Tours' articles published in the Manchester City News in 1902, was the founding of the Manchester Pedestrian Club. The Club's first walk was made on 11th July 1903. It was from Hayfield to Castleton in the Peak District, by way of Hope. In all there were nine walks in their first season. The longest, and most famous of these was their 'Championship March' from Manchester to Nantwich in mid-Cheshire, a distance of forty miles, which was made along roads, not footpaths!

Not content with this relatively modest achievement, the following year they set themselves the task of walking from Manchester to London, a distance of 188 miles in just five days. Not surprisingly, this brave venture excited a great deal of interest, to the extent that a fit and courageous reporter from the Manchester Guardian elected to walk the whole distance with them. Thankfully, he made it to the bitter end, whilst also finding the time and energy to telegraph a report on the progress of the march each day. (8)

Coverage of the event also appeared in no less than twenty London and provincial papers.

With much cheering and waving the intrepid band set out at 1 p.m. on Saturday 21st May 1904. The six blistered and weary survivors of this epic endurance test staggered up to Marble Arch, London, at 5.30 p.m. on Thursday 26th May, just thirty minutes over the ambitious target they had set themselves of completing the full trek in just five days. Interestingly, this venture actually served as an inspiration to succeeding members, for after this the Club organised many long-distance treks, which included their famous Manchester to Bristol walk, undertaken in 1907, which took seven days, and two walks to Paris, once from Boulogne and once from Dieppe. The Club also did many local walks, to the extent that by the end of 1937 they had completed 1,446 rambles, largely in the Manchester and surrounding areas. (9)

The Young Naturalists League. This League, closely associated with the London Ramblers' Federation, was founded in April 1909, as a direct result of the growing interest taken in natural history and country pursuits by the rising generation. Perhaps, or partly because, there was no charge for membership, the organisation grew rapidly. As early as 1915 about 7,000 boys and girls had enrolled as members. When joining each youngster was obliged to make a few simple pledges, after which they were presented with a nicely designed badge at less than cost price.

In 1915 there were 50 branches of the League at home and abroad. Most of these held indoor meetings during the winter, and went on rambles in the summer. Each branch was expected to send in 'Reports' to H.Q. from time to time, which was based at 8 Southampton Street, Strand, London. The Hon. Sec. at this time was W. Percival Westell. It was, of course, not only youngsters who were interested in combining rambling and natural history during the closing decades of the 19th and the early decades of the

20th Century. For instance, in 1915, the Birkbeck College Natural History Society, was affiliated to the London based Ramblers' Federation, as was the British Empire Naturalists' Association. (10) The 'Hazards' of embarking on a day's sketching, with a Field Naturalist Rambling Group in 1887, is brilliantly portrayed by an artist from the *Graphic* on the following page. (11)

Other established Clubs in existence in the London area in the first decades of the 20th Century include the **Chums Rambling Group,** who organised country rambles on alternative Sundays. Ladies and gentlemen who were desirous of joining this Club were invited to communicate with the Hon. Secretary – Mrs W.J. Talbot, 20 Manor Park London. Another notable London Group was the **Crofton Park Ramblers,** who met regularly at The Brockley Jack Hotel. Subscription was set at 1s per annum.

We are, however, assured that in 1915 the premier North London group was the **Highbury United Rambling Club.** To attract potential members the public was told that the club was open to either sex, the company was good and they had interesting rambles. The **Harringay Conservatives Al-Frescoes Group** was run by Mr Rafferty, whilst a Mr Smart was leader of the **Heathen Rambling Club**!

Perhaps one of the best known pioneer rambling groups in London was the **Ranken Rambling Club.** First established in 1897, it was renamed in 1905. "Ladies and Gentlemen desiring interesting country rambles in cheery company are invited to apply for particulars of the above club, which will be gladly supplied by Mr Claude G. Gentry, Hon. Secretary." In notices advertising the Club Mr Gentry also drew attention to other matters relating to the Club, namely: "This is one of the few Clubs with open membership, i.e., not connected with any society or organisation. Rambles are arranged for alternative Saturday afternoons and on Bank Holidays". (12)

A Day's Sketching with the Field Naturalist, 1887

Beautiful scenery was to be enjoyed by all these pioneering London groups, in the nearby Home Counties. As the illustration on the following page indicates, they would also have had the chance to cast their eyes on strange local events, as they passed through old-world villages! These rambles also gave local Equestrians the opportunity of looking down on pedestrians, both from their high position in Society, and their lofty perches on horse back – as they passed each other, likes ships in the night, on the dusty highways and byeways.

Equestrians v. Pedestrians

A day in the country

It is also interesting to note that from the first decades of the 20th Century all these pioneering groups, affiliated to a 'Federation,' were able to take advice from, and submit items for publication to their respective 'Handbook' Editor. Some of the items published were instructive, others amusing and, looking back from our point in time, many managed to be both at the same time. Although, it has to be said, that was clearly not the intention of the writers at the time!

One such item, published in 1914, stated that the first thought that rises in the mind when planning an 'excursion' was what to take. "Luggage" – that heterogeneous collection of impedimenta beloved by the average holiday-maker was "taboo." The writer then assured readers that a *small* haversack packed with a few essentials, was all they required. Among the obvious items they were advised to take was a pair of strong boots, a waterproof coat or cape, and 'Night Attire'. More interestingly, however, they were then told that 'Knickers' are preferable to trousers, as permitting 'freer use of the legs." Regarding provisions, the writer then concluded with the following words of wisdom which, I suspect, were often disregarded: " Spirits and other alcoholic liquors are best avoided during the walk, such being partaken of, if tastes lie in that direction, in the evening. On a hot day, indulging in liquids of any sort only leads to excessive perspiration, frequently without quenching the thirst at all, so that moderation is the wisest course". (13)

The following song, re-published in 1914, also catches the spirit of the very early pioneer walkers, although, today, perhaps not quite in the way the author intended! It was written about 1874 by Dr. Leslie of Perth, and later culled from a collection compiled for school use by a Committee of the Perth Branch of the Educational Institute of Scotland. The Editor of *The Rambler's Yearbook*, 1914, added: "We do not know if the book is still in circulation; but in any case we make no apology for reproducing a song which should appeal to every Rambler".

THE FOOT TRAVELLER'S SONG

On foot I gaily take my way,
    Hurrah!
O'er mountains bare and meadow's gay,
    Hurrah !
And he who is not of my mind,
Another travelling mate may find,
He cannot go with me,
    Hurrah! Tra la la la la la !

No snail-paced friend I want, not I !,
　　Hurrah!
At every step to pause and sigh,
　　Hurrah !
No gloomy man to scowl or grown,
And over others' sins make moan;
I'd rather trudge alone.
　　Hurrah ! tra la la la la la

Foot-travel to the gay is sweet,
　　Hurrah !
But heavy hearts make heavy feet,
　　Hurrah
The man who loves the sunshine bright,
And never peeps behind for night,
That is the man for me.
　　Hurrah ! tra la la la la la !　　　　(14)

Don't forget that you are a gentleman! From time to time the great Lawrence W. Chubb, Secretary of the Commons and Footpaths Preservation Society, made contributions to The Rambler's Handbook. Among Chubb's more notable items was one that appeared in 1914 under the heading of **"Some Don'ts."** Here he opened by offering standard advise about closing gates, not leaving litter, making sure not to frighten animals, and making sure not to picnic in hayfields. However, he then concluded with these memorable, paternalistic words: "…and what may be deemed appropriate enough at Hampstead Heath on a Bank Holiday is out of place elsewhere. In short, *Don't forget that you are a Gentleman, when all the rest of this small catalogue of "don'ts" will prove unnecessary"*. (Lawrence Chubb) (15)

142

SOME INCIDENTS OF A WALKING TOUR

The above illustration indicates the sort of incidents that the pioneer ramblers might have encountered on one of their "Walking Tours."

143

As the century moved on, past the bloody years of the Great War, more and more rambling clubs became established in various parts of the country. Foremost among these were the many groups that were set up on Merseyside, where urbanised people, from medical practitioners and solicitors, to clerks and shop assistants, took to rambling to escape their dull urban existence. The nearby mountains of North Wales, which they often referred to, with affection, as 'Merseyside's Mountains' appeared regularly as a favourite destination on their respective walks programmes.

There is, of course, a sound historical basis for this affinity with Wales on Merseyside. Namely, because Liverpool, nearby Wallasey, meaning, in Welsh, 'Hill of the Welsh, and Birkenhead, were all, to a very appreciable extend, built by the Welsh and, down to the present day, this great conurbation is still heavily populated by the immediate descendants of the Welsh who moved to Merseyside. In point of fact, so great was this affinity that up until recently Liverpool was often referred to, with an equal degree of affection, by the Welsh, as the Capital of Wales.

However, to defend the interests of the large number of rambling groups already in existence on Merseyside in the 1920's, The Liverpool and District Ramblers' Federation was established. The first of their famous *Ramblers' Handbooks* appeared in 1926. Many rambling groups in the area then affiliated to the Federation making it, along with Manchester, Sheffield and London, one of the most influential Federations in Britain. Among the Clubs affiliated to the Federation, at this time, several are particularly notable, and deserve a special mention.

Firstly, there was the **'As-You-Like-It-Club** whose aims were clear and simple, namely, "To provide opportunities for social enjoyment by the organisation of rambles, socials etc". Meetings were held once a month. They had socials in the winter, and rambles in the summer. The **Speedwell Ramblers** put the emphasis on being interested in nature and the open air. The **5th Birkenhead (H.Q.) Rover Troop** stated that their aim was to promote the outdoor life among youths and men above the age of seventeen and, as one might expect, being the Scouts, cycling, camping, trekking, and playing games, also featured on their action-packed, character-building agenda.

By way of contrast, the **Liverpool Botanical Society** had a far more sedate and intellectual programme than most of the other Clubs. Based at Hartley's Laboratories, the objects of this pioneering group was "To stimulate and promote the various branches of botany, to bring to local workers, students, and those interested in the subject into contact, and for mutual assistance, and to encourage original work and research.". Here, as will be noted, no mention was made of 'rambling' as such, although they did go so far as to hold 'Field Meetings' during the summer.

The Liverpool Fabian Society was also affiliated to the Federation, though they made no pretence of being interested in rambling! To compensate, however, they did have lectures on a Friday. Their stated objects were "Socialisation of the essentials of Civilisation.". Established in 1884, they famously based their philosophy on the slowly, slowly tactics of the Roman General Fabius Maximus. (Whether or not they carried this philosophy over into their mode of progression on an occasional stroll is not recorded!)

The Vegetarian Cycling and Athletic Club (Liverpool Branch) (Motto- Feed Well, Speed Well) had its Headquarters at 54 Whitechapel. Subscriptions were 2/6 (non-active) and 5/0 (active). Rambling, Cycling, Running, Race-walking, Swimming and Tennis all featured on the agenda of this super-fit Club. In Wallasey there were four affiliates, namely, the **Wallasey Amateur Photographic Society,** who did not formally include rambling among its activities. **The Wallasey Independent Labour Party** whose stated aims was

"To propagate the principle of socialism" – and go for walks on Sunday afternoons!

The **Wallasey Rambling Club** went on rambles every other week – summer *and* winter. They also held socials in winter. A Miss Prudence was the Hon. Secretary. The stated objects of the Club sounded particularly pleasant: "To promote friendships in their highest sense, and enable members to enjoy the open air and observe the beauties of nature". Last but not least, was the **Wirral Group** whose entry, I think, deserves to be quoted in full, for today the **Wirral Group of the Ramblers' Association** is the 2nd largest in the United Kingdom.

The Wirral Ramblers, Wallasey, Cheshire.

Objects – To promote social acquaintance and spirit of comradeship among its members. *President,* Councillor J.B. Jones; *Chairman of Committee,* Geo. J. Warren; *Hon. Treasurer*, Miss M. A. Holt; *Hon. Secretary,* L. Ditchfield, 53 Borrowdale Road, Sefton Park, Liverpool. Rambles in summer. Socials, Whist Drives, Dances, 1st Friday in each month at Liverpool and Wallasey in Winter. Subscription 2/6. (16)

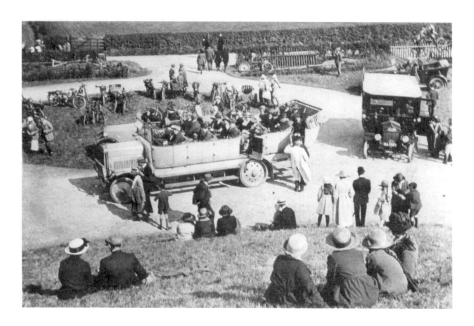

In the 1920's people from the cities were able to reach the country by charabanc, such as the one illustrated above. Llangollen, it is interesting to note, was the destination of the world's first charabanc trip in 1906. (The vehicle was hired by eighteen members of the Liverpool Bowling Club)

CHAPTER TWELVE   THE NINETEEN THIRTIES

Above all others Dr. Cyril Edwin Mitchinson Joad serves as a prime example of the spirit of the rambling movement in the 1930's. Born in 1891 he was educated at Tiverton and Balliol College Oxford. He began his long career with the Board of Trade in 1914. In 1930, however, he left the Ministry to become Head of the Department of Philosophy at Birkbeck College, University of London. A leading light in the rambling movement for many years, he was destined to become a regular speaker at the famous Winnats Pass Access Rallies during the 1930's. (1) A short extract from an article he wrote in 1932 indicates just how popular rambling had become with young people in the 1930's – and particularly in the North of England:

"Those of us who live in the south have little conception of the hold which the 'rambling' movement has upon the young people of the north. The Central Station at Manchester early on a Sunday morning is an unforgettable sight. With its crowds of ramblers, complete with ruck-sacks, shorts and hobnailed boots, waiting for a train to Edale, Chinley, Castleton and the Derbyshire moors, it might lead one to suppose that the whole of Manchester was in exodus. And it is, indeed true that this generation has replaced beer by 'hiking' as the shortest cut out of Manchester." (2)

The first of four well-known books that Joad wrote about the countryside and rambling was *The Horrors of the Countryside,* which, it is interesting to note, was published in 1931 by the celebrated left-wing, political duo, Leonard and Virginia Woolf, at their Hogarth Press. Both were supporters of the Fabian Society, and Virginia, the famous novelist and critic was, it should be noted, the second daughter of Sir Leslie Stephen, founder of the aforementioned 'Sunday Tramps'. (3)

Combined Rail and Walking Tours were organised in many parts of
Britain by the Railways during the first part of the 20th Century.
This advert. appeared in the "Ramblers' Handbook, 1931.

   Throughout the 1930's, however, Joad's books – and indeed
many others – continued to popularise rambling and also focus
attention on the 'Access' problems facing the ever increasing army
of ramblers. Thousands were taking to the hills, and the published
works on the subject were offering free advice, on every possible
aspect of this leisure pursuit. In 1927, for instance, Stephen Graham
published his notable work *The Gentle Art of Tramping*. In this
well-known book, among many other things, he found space to offer
invaluable tips on walking attire!

149

It was, he felt, a mistake to take to the countryside clad in new plus-fours, sports jacket, West-End tie, jewelled tie-pin, or in gaiters, or carrying a silver-topped cane. Sober, tough walking gear should be the order of the day and, most importantly, strong boots with very substantial soles. His philosophical observations on rambling are revealing, insofar as they present an insight into the assumed higher status of an urban worker to that of a rural gardener – the latter, apparently, being expected to touch his forelock to the former, under normal, non-rambling circumstances!

"What a relief to cease being for a while a grade-three clerk, or grade two clerk who has reached his limit, to cease to be identified by one's salary or by one's golf handicap. It is undoubtedly a delicious moment when Miles the gardener, seeing you come along in tramping rig omits to touch his hat as you pass. Of course it is part of the gentle art not to be offended. It is no small part of the gentle art of tramping to learn to accept the simple and humble role and not crave respect, honour, obeisance." (4)

During the 1930's the media played a significant role in popularising rambling. Articles on the subject appearing regularly in such papers as *The Manchester Evening Chronicle,* the *Manchester Guardian, The Times,* and many others up and down the country. Like the author Stephen Graham they also offered much advice on what to wear when out walking. Typical of these was an Article which appeared in the Manchester press in the spring of 1932, which, it is interesting to note, was aimed at the growing number of female ramblers.

Hiking, the writer felt, was such a popular way of spending a weekend that it was worth while making sure one had the right sort of clothes. Tweed skirts (which fitted neatly round the hips) Shetland woollen jumpers, and a costume coat, that matched the skirt, all met with approval. Potential female hikers were also advised to take a medium weight mackintosh, 'sensible' shoes, and a little crocheted or knitted beret, because they offered little resistance to the wind, and could easily be carried in the pocket while the hair is being given a sun and breeze treatment. (5)

Two years later the great artist, William Russell Flint (later Sir William) again took up the issue of 'Hikers' dress for, it would seem, only a minority were taking a lead from the aforementioned, fashion orientated writer on rambling. In an impassioned letter to *The Times*, which appeared under the sub-heading "Plea for Gayer Garments – Homely Cheeks and Skinny Legs," Flint posed the profound question: "Why do our lean-limbed young men and shapely damsels make themselves so ugly in potato colour and khaki while merely taking a walk?" The Editor responded, tongue-in-cheek, by suggesting that Flint himself should make efforts to change things by putting a picture in next year's Royal Academy Exhibition of a group of hikers dressed as he would have them dressed, then 'khaki and potato' would surely be doomed for ever. (6)

Morality was also an issue to be taken into account! Under the banner headline 'Is Hiking Morally Dangerous' that appeared in the Y.H.A. periodical in 1936, the Rev. Dick Sheppard did his best to re-assure anxious parents on this crucial issue. There was, he had to concede, moral dangers in hiking but added – just as there are in everything else. He continued "I'll admit right away that, when young men and girls go hiking together, they may find opportunities for immorality. But these won't tempt anyone who doesn't want to be tempted... The letters I received on this subject were from people who are still living in the Victorian age. I don't take them seriously."

All in all, Sheppard felt, "Hikers are a decent lot. You have only to talk to them to realise that". He concluded by stating that vigorous outdoor exercise is in itself a way of keeping moral, as well as physical health. "There's nuthin like work to take the devil out o' ee". an old countryman once said to me. And a vigorous day's walking, if it isn't exactly work, still leaves the body healthily tired. It "takes the devil out of 'ee." (7)

Wayfaring Holidays in Scotland

The 'Hiking Boom' of the 1930's also gave a tremendous boost to the commercial and non-commercial hostel and hiking-related tourist industry. In Scotland Tom S. Hall's Wayfaring Holidays Organisation offered a programme of walks based on Scotland, with other low cost ventures in North Wales, Devon and all parts of the Continent. Charges were from £4 upwards. (8) Fred Tallant ran the Ardlington Touring Club from his office at 11 Lincoln's Inn Fields in London. From his base in the capital he organised walking tours in Switzerland, Norway and the Dolomites,

152

as well as offering his speciality for the more affluent – a "Round the World" Tour! (9)

In 1932 the 'Comradeship' Holiday Group was thriving. With a Head Office in Birmingham, they also had a local group based on Waterloo, Liverpool and, no doubt, many other places. They had two centres in North Wales, which were open all the year round, and summer centres at Oban, the Lake District, Whitby, Ramsey and many other places. (10) By regular adverts placed in the 'Out-of-Doors' press 'Trampers' and Cyclists were advised that 'International Tramping Tours' of Leeds had over fifty tours on offer, with prices from £3.15s for 6 days.

A "Comradeship" Holiday is the Holiday for You! (1932)

This section would, of course, not be complete without paying some attention to the "The "F.H.A." – 'The Friendship Holiday Association' run by H.Y.C. White from his Headquarters: Heathmount Hall, Ilkley Moors, Yorkshire.   In 1927 the F.H.A. were advertising guest-house accommodation at Anglesey, North Berwick, Bournemouth and seven other places. (11)   However, by 1928 they were advertising holidays based on 13 'Centres' (12) which rose to 19 'Centres' by 1932. (13)

F.H.A. HOLIDAYS
ARE GREAT

STEEPHILL CASTLE, VENTNOR, ISLE OF WIGHT.

F. (Friendship
H. (Holidays
A. (Association

Headquarters :
HEATHMOUNT HALL.
ILKLEY MOORS, Yorks.
Telephone : 490.
Write for Syllabus.

PRINCIPAL - HY. C. WHITE.

CENTRES :—
ILKLEY MOOR.
NORTH BERWICK, Scotland.
GLYN GARTH, Anglesey.
PENMAENMAWR, N. Wales.
BOURNEMOUTH, S. Coast.
AMBLESIDE, Lake District.
ISLE OF MAN.
VENTNOR, Isle of Wight.
PAIGNTON.
SALTBURN, Yorkshire Coast.
ARDENTINNY, nr. Dunoon.
SEAFORD BAY, Eastbourne.
BRAY, Wicklow, Ireland.
LONDON and BRUGES.
BLACKPOOL.
FILEI.
PWLLHELI.
CONWAY.

"F.H.A. Holidays are Great"

154

The Co-operative Holiday Association and the Holiday Fellowship. The old-established Co-operative Holiday Association, and the closely related Holiday Fellowship were both well to the fore in benefiting from the rush of interest in hiking in the 1930's. Both were also to remain organisations of lasting significance in the history of the rambling movement. The Co-operative Holiday Association was founded in 1893 and the Holiday Fellowship in 1913. The 'Prime Mover' in both ventures was T. Arthur Leonard, Congregational Minister of the bleak upland township of Colne in North Lancashire. Leonard, who has been christened the father of the open air movement was, in turn, greatly influenced by the ideals of the co-operative movement.

The inhabitants of this part of Lancashire, in the late-Victorian era, were, like Tom Stephenson, leading light of the rambling movement for many years – hard working mill-folk. When the 'Wakes' week came round each year there was, as T.A. Leonard put it – "a general exodus down the long road to the station where the town well-nigh emptied its population into trains that carried people to Blackpool and Morecombe, the more prosperous journeying as far afield as Douglas". (14)

All of which prompted Leonard to consider setting up a holiday organisation that would have something more challenging to offer working people, as an alternative to the routine, annual family pilgrimage to the sea-side. As a start he set up a Colne-based rambling club. This venture was actually part of the Social Guild work of a Congregational Church in Colne, of which Leonard was the Minister. On behalf of this club Leonard planned a Guild Holiday at Ambleside in June, 1891.

Holidays of this type then became an annual event. In 1893 his club was at Keswick, in the heart of the Lake District and, in the same year, Leonard formed the Co-operative Holidays Association. Within a short space of time the C.H.A. opened 'Abbey Guest

House' at Whitby and, soon after that 'Friedensthal' at Scalby was opened. From this modest start the C.H.A. expanded rapidly until, by the 1930's, the organisation was able to offer cost-effective holidays in all parts of Britain and, as far afield as Germany and Switzerland on the continent.

A typical C.H.A. advertisement of the inter-war period

156

Notwithstanding the early success of the C.H.A. in 1913 Leonard established the Holiday Fellowship out of the Co-operative Holiday Association. The idea being to extend the work begun twenty years ago by this first organisation, and because he, and others, felt that it was not quite fulfilling the ideals upon which it was founded. However, Leonard and his colleagues made it clear that the new Fellowship was not intended to be a competitor of the C.H.A., but a *companion* organisation, pioneered by an old group of C.H.A. friends. The main area of concern of this group was that the parent organisation had not been making enough progress in international work, a deficit they intended to correct via the new sister organisation. In certain other ways the new body also diverged from the model of the C.H.A. – notably by having a Co-operative form of organisation. (15)

The two most significant developments in the history of the rambling movement, however, were to take place in the 1930's. The first was the establishment in 1930 of the Youth Hostel Association in Britain. The second was the founding of the Ramblers' Association in 1935. The Youth Hostel movement first appeared in Britain as 'The International Youth Tramps'. Writing late in 1930, Ingram Knowles, then Joint Secretary International Youth Tramps, and Hon. Treasurer of the British Youth Hostels Association, urged young people to look to Germany – a land he described as a Ramblers Paradise – for inspiration. (16)

Meanwhile, in 1934, just one year before the Ramblers' Federations joined forces and became the Ramblers' Association, co-operation was already in hand between the hostel and rambling movements. Under the name of the Hostel Builders' Society, a Youth Hostel was established at Llangollen, which became known as The Ramblers' Hostel. It was officially handed over to the Youth Hostels Association on Saturday 6th May, at a gathering of Officers of the Association and the Liverpool and District Ramblers'

Federation, together with members of the Llangollen Urban District Council. (17)

The Hiking craze of the 1930's was at its zenith, when political storm clouds were gathering once more over Europe. One of the reasons that rambling was so popular with young people at this time was, undoubtedly, because the railway system was both efficient and cheap. Buses had also made their appearance, which made access to the countryside even more easy. The 'Hungry Thirties' were a dreadful reality to those without work, but the fortunate ones in employment had time and money to get out into the countryside at the weekends.

German ideology had also wafted across the channel. 'Youth' itself, under the influence of Germany ideology, had become 'fashionable.' A 'return to nature' – in a Wagnerian sense – had been placed on an ideological pedestal. It was also a world in which cheap flights to the bars and beaches of the Canary Islands, or Southern Spain, did not exist, to act as a lure to tempt young people away from the hills and valleys of their native island.

From the Cover of Y.H.A. "Rucksack" February 1936

158

Mr T. Arthur Leonard in 1932
Founder of the Co-operative Holidays Association.
Founder of the Holiday Fellowship.
President of the Liverpool and District Ramblers' Federation.
Chairman of the National Council of Ramblers' Federations.

CHAPTER THIRTEEN
THE YOUTH HOSTEL MOVEMENT

The 'Hiking Boom' of the 1930's also brought with it the demand for cheap accommodation in the countryside. Unfortunately, the Inns, pubs and farms of this period did not cater for poor, young walkers. Broadly speaking hotels and pubs fell into two classes. Expensive hotels designed to cater for motorists and, pubs which sold food and drink, but had very limited accommodation. In general, the proprietors of such establishments, particularly the former, also tended to look askance at the rucksacks and muddy boots of the young hikers. In addition to this, farms willing to take in stray walkers, or cyclists, were not easy to find. It was against this background that the Youth Hostel Association was formally established in Britain in 1930 in order to fill the breach by providing cheap 'Sanctuaries for Ramblers'. (1)

Informally, however, things had started to move before 1930. In the South-west Mr. Ralph Gardiner had already organised the Wessex Hikers' Lodges. By 1929 'The Northumbrian Trampers Guild' had seven centres up and running, and they in turn had made reciprocal arrangements with the Scottish Young Men's Holiday Fellowship for the use of each other's accommodation. (2)

However, to understand the history of the Youth Hostel Movement we must go back to Germany where the movement began. Firstly, we must note, the German Youth Movement was in existence long before there was a Hitler, or even the conception of a political 'movement' as a specific function of an elite within, and operating as a function of oppression against the masses. Nevertheless, a particular characteristic of early 20th Century 'Germanism' was presented as a movement of youth against all that had decayed and become obsolete. (3)

160

What were the social and political conditions that gave birth to a phenomena that was to become the 'Free German Youth Movement'? Essentially, the German Youth Movement, before the 1914–1918 war was the protest of the youth of the middle-classes against the mentality, customs and practices of their own class. At this time the social life of the German bourgeoisie was, to a significant degree, determined by very conventional forms.

The aim of the school in Germany was, above all else, the inculcation of blind obedience upon the child. Every possibility of a person forming his own ideas, of individual development, was systematically crushed. As the German anti-fascist writer Karl Otten put it in 1942, "The curriculum was permeated with a rigid and one-sided nationalism and with glorification of things military: soldiers and officials were exalted beings; obedience to them was the essence of German Life". (4)

It was a society that was heavily influenced by a peculiarly Nordic brand of 'Romanticism', which mode of thinking tends to idealise the experience and facts of nature and life, and is thus the opposite of realism. The tendency is hard to define, at least concisely. Nevertheless, it can, perhaps, be quickly summarised as a philosophical cocktail, heavily laced with notions of 'Nordic' superiority; tales of the wondrous doings of Teutonic Knights; the glorification of German 'Folk' activity, 'Youth' and, by way of a reaction against industrialisation, a call for a 'Return to Nature', albeit via a very dimly-lit ideological trail!

At the root of this heady brew was a disturbingly gruesome, and totally unrealistic glorification of war, notably due to the influence of the early German 'Romantic' Bernd Heinrich Wilhelm von Kleist. It is, as Rohan Butler rightly pointed out in 1941, rather disconcerting to find Kleist, way back in 1809, writing *Germania an ihre Kinder (Germany to Her Children)* for of all the many German battle-songs it is, perhaps the most terrible in its sheer delight in

161

carnage. In which, for example, Kleist thunders: *Stehst du auf, Germania? Ist der Tag Rache ?* (*Is there a day of vengeance?*). (5)

Education in this rigidly authoritarian state was also, by custom and practice, inseparable from 'encouragement' by blows. Small wonder then that in later life, the man, who, as a child was beaten in turn once he was grown up, invariably had a strong, irrational urge to take vengeance on others. It was, of course, this psychical interaction which invested the German soldier with a will to fight, to defeat the enemy, to annihilate him. The sensitive ones, understandably, tended to break down under this twin onslaught of indoctrination and maltreatment.

Consequently, from early in the 19th Century the German youth began to protest vehemently against these oppressive conditions, choosing, as the first platform, the organised *Burschenschaften* – that is the University Students Associations. This long, ongoing historical experience sank deep into the mind of the German youth, which eventually emerged in the shape of a wide "Movement of the Youthful Masses" which aroused, in turn, astonishment, fear, and eventually abhorrence.

Enter the Wandervogel. As a reaction against this oppression in the last years of the 19th Century the need for a more natural, less oppressive, simple and harmonious life-style was felt by some of the pupils of a grammar school (Gymnasium) in Steglitz, near Berlin. They decided to walk in their leisure-time in the local countryside and, to spend their holidays walking through the hills and forests. At first these walks were not very different from their usual school walks, but then they began to take things more seriously. They bought suitable clothing for their expeditions, took a dim view of alcohol and tobacco, and formed a Walking Fellowship, the 'Wandervogel' – Wandering Bird, Bird of Passage, which formed the foundation on which the German rambling and hostel movements were built. (6)

Boys, and at a later date girls, joined this new movement in droves and, as in Britain, began to head for the countryside. However, overnight accommodation, on long treks presented problems for the organisers. With no cheap hostels available they met this challenge in the following manner. At sunset the practice was to go to a farmer and ask if he would allow them to sleep in his barn! The usual method of payment was a "Joyful Song" which was calculated to gain the farmer's consent! In fact, singing featured prominently on the action-packed agenda of most Wandervogel groups. To cater for this a collection of old folk songs was published called the "Zupfgeigen-Hansl" which became the most popular community song book in the German Youth Movement. These young people also paid a great deal of attention to folk-dance. (7)

The origins of the Federation of German Youth Hostels. Meanwhile, country walks by school children, led by a teacher, remained part of the German school curriculum. These walks often varied between an afternoon picnic in the woods in term time to a fortnight's tramp in the holidays across country. Richard Schirrman, a teacher in a Westphalian elementary school, had proved the benefits of such trips in his own class, but he was troubled by the lack of accommodation at night time for his groups. He responded to this challenge in 1909. In a letter to the local newspaper he suggested that school premises should be made available for this purpose in the holidays. By way of a response, however, a small house in Altema was put at his disposal and, in 1910, this was opened as the first real "Youth Hostel."

Progress was extraordinarily rapid. By 1911 there were 17 hostels, which rose to 200 by 1914, 700 by 1920 and 2,320 by 1932. However, it is interesting to note that in 1913 – just prior to the First World War – the growing movement in various parts of the country was rapidly converted into the *Verband fuer deutsche*

Jugendherbergen   (Federation of German Youth Hostels), commonly known as "D.J.H." Richard Schirrman became the first General Secretary of the new Federation. Support flooded in from many town councils and other organisations. More 'heavyweight' backing then followed from the German Ministry of the interior, the Prussian Ministry of Education and the Governments of most of the German provinces. In addition, Churches, Trade Unions and others all gave the movement moral and material support.

Unfortunately, the National Socialist Youth Organisation was formed by Adolf Hitler in 1922. It's stated aim was the 'regeneration' of the German people! Along with the Party it was banned for a while, but within a few short years the *Hitlerjugend* was to become the sole organisation of German youth. (8) Backed by big business, Hitler was indeed on the move. During 1929 the sales of his tedious work *Mein Kampf* more than doubled. (8)

Germany, the pioneer nation of youth-hostelling, under the ever-increasing influence of Adolph Hitler, was heading for the wrong ideological port. Nevertheless, during the 1920's the D.J.H. still had a unique value in bringing together young people of all political and religious beliefs. Meanwhile, following the 1st World War, hostile attitudes in Britain towards Germany were slowly starting to evaporate. The British were re-discovering Germany. What is more, many of these visitors were young, were staying in German Youth Hostels, and bringing back favourable reports about them. At the close of 1929 the D.J.H. had 700 British members. In this notable year of 1929 the British Federation of Youth was re-constituted as The British Youth Council. Establishment of a nation-wide chain of Youth Hostels was high on their agenda. A provisional committee was set up, then, in September 1929, the Liverpool Ramblers' Federation gave strong support to this development. (9)

The Liverpool and District Ramblers' Federation had before it a resolution that called for the creation of a chain of 'Shelters' that would run from Arrowe Park, Birkenhead, to Beaumaris. The long route was to run via proposed hostels at Mold, Llangollen, Devil's Bridge, Morfa and Snowdon, at which young ramblers could obtain a night's shelter at a charge of six pence! The ambitious schedule before them on 30th September 1929 was that the scheme could be up and running by summer 1930. The strategy was that that facilities might be offered by "existing associations with headquarters at the different centres mentioned". The article covering the issue in the Liverpool press then made it clear that the inspiration for this project had come directly from Germany.

"Mr T. F. Fairclough, a member of the Liverpool Committee who has returned from a tour of Germany, told the Daily Post representative that the experience had made him very enthusiastic about starting a similar scheme in England [which] eventually may be given government aid." The reporter concluded: "Mr Fairclough and Mr. A Embleton, Secretary of the Federation both pointed out that the scheme was not only to provide cheap lodgings, but was an important branch of the World Federation of Youth". (10)

An interesting affinity with the Scout movement, hostels and rambling now emerges. A clue to this is the proposed staring point for the chain of hostels, Arrowe Park, Birkenhead, and an article published by the Federation, offering their support to the organisers of the world-famous Scout Jamboree, which also took place in Birkenhead in 1929.

"The organisers of the Scout Jamboree to be held in Arrowe Park, Birkenhead in August 1929 approached your committee with the suggestion that the Federation should provide leaders for parties of scouts attending the Jamboree desiring to explore the Wirral Peninsula. The committee decided to give the scheme their fullest support as they feel confident that leaders of local rambling clubs and others would be glad of an opportunity of giving their services in such interesting work." (11)

In the autumn of 1930 the Lord Mayor of Liverpool, Mr Lawrence Holt, himself a keen walker and climber, called a town hall meeting. Notable 'Godparents' came forward and endowed each proposed hostel with £300. The plan was that the hostels themselves would not be very pretentious, although each would be fitted with a well-equipped kitchen and modern conveniences. It was also agreed that great care would be taken with the design of the buildings so that they would harmonise with the natural beauties around them. (12)

One was the Old School at Cyffylliog, beyond Ruthin. Another was the 'Pilkington' Hostel at Plas-yn-Cornel, Llansannan, a house deep in a valley of the Denbighshire moors. The third was Gwydyr Ucha, the 'Stuart Downs' Hostel, near the river Conwy. The fourth was Idwal Cottage, a climbing centre at the head of the Nant Ffrancon, which was let to the Association at a nominal rent by Lord Penrhyn. In 1931 the 'Holt Hostel' was opened at Maeshafn, near Mold. Still in use today, it was designed by the celebrated architect, Clough Williams-Ellis.

A National Association was formed in 1930, and by 1932 there were local branches of the organisation in all parts of Britain, controlling the organisation of 73 Hostels in England and Wales. At the same time chains of Hostels was also being set up in Scotland and Ireland. (13) Looking back on these early days Alf Embleton, leading light of the rambling and hostel movement, made an interesting observation about the aims and objectives of the hostel movement. He began by citing a 1929 report on the movement that appeared in the Daily News of 28th September 1929:

'Waysmeet' Hostel, All Saints' Lane, Canterbury.

The 'Waysmeet' Hostel, All Saints' Lane, Canterbury

"We want somewhere young people can go and be free to talk and think in their own way. The idea is to live simply and to tramp about, to sleep on a palliasse rather than a bed and to use enamelled mugs and plates rather than china." Alf then added: "That seems to indicate a desire for discomfort for the sake of discomfort, a spirit which is not entirely dead in the Y.H.A. even 21 years later".

The underlying 'spirit' of the movement, however, still remained firmly rooted in the Germany ideology of the period, which goes a long way to explain this penchant for a spartan, almost militaristic tendency within the Y.H.A. In 1936 Dr. Goebbels introduced the 'Strength through Joy' programme, which was run in conjunction with a 'Labour Service' programme aimed at getting youngsters back into Hitler's version of a 'healthy' relationship with nature.

This, of course, not by rambling and spending holidays in ordinary youth hostels, but by working for up to six hours a day as unpaid agricultural or forestry labourers in special, army style camps. Here, in these establishments, an effort to transfer well-disciplined firing-trench unity into the 'trench camaraderie of swamp and moor' was the order of the day. (14)

Nevertheless, in 1936, when Hitler was tightening his ideological and political grip on Germany, the British Government felt compelled to send a committee to Germany to report on the 'Strength through Joy' initiative. Significantly, the King's speech of 1936 contained a promise of a Bill to improve the physical condition of the Nation. Keeping youngsters in hostels and out rambling not only improved the health of youngsters, it also kept them well away from politics! The political pundits were, however, pushing on an open door, for urban youngsters, throughout the twenties and the thirties, were having a long, ongoing love affair with the 'Great Outdoors.'

The concept of youth hostels, without the underlying political scheming of the period, filled a gap. It was the right idea, at the right time, and youngsters took to them like ducks take to water. By the end of 1932 membership had increased from 1,165 to 3,873. The following year brought further increases in membership, moving up to 7,082. And during this hectic year no less than 17 new hostels were opened, and this included the first town hostel, at Edinburgh. The Y.H.A. was on its way, destined to become the international entity we all know and love today.

In the early days the British Youth Hostel movement such rapid growth would not have been possible without serious financial support. So who were the backers? Among others it was the Carnegie Trust. Just two years after the Association was set up this Trust gave the Association a very substantial sum, part of which went towards the establishment of model hostels. About the same time the National Trust placed at the disposal of the Y.H.A. the Winchester City Mill – and several other properties.

Later, as Barclay Baron pointed out in 1936, the Y.H.A. was "nobly befriended" by the King George V Jubilee Trust, the sum received being sufficient to pay for about six new hostels. The Commissioners for the 'Special Areas' also made impressive grants to enable hostels to be established and used by the young people in the districts hardest hit by unemployment. (15)

Today, in the 21st Century, the YHA retains formal links with the RA. Affiliated to the Ramblers' Association at national level, it is one of eleven national organisations to maintain fraternal relations with the RA at this level. (16)

The Glen Nevis Youth Hostel – one of the first to be opened by the Scottish YHA

CHAPTER FOURTEEN   THE RAMBLERS' ASSOCIATION

In previous chapters the history of just a few of the more notable late 19th and early 20th century rambling clubs has been outlined. These, however, merely serve as examples, for in the face of escalating urbanisation the same period also saw an ever-increasing number of people turning to the countryside for their rest and recreation. During these years rambling clubs were established at a truly remarkable rate. With this upsurge of interest also came the realisation that the right to walk on footpaths and bridleways and, in the future, perhaps, gain open access on mountains and moors, had to be protected and, in the case of the latter, campaigned for.

As already noted, the first federation of rambling clubs took place in Glasgow, with the formation of the West of Scotland Ramblers' Alliance in 1892, which was followed by the establishment of the larger and more influential London based Federation of Rambling Clubs in 1905. Federations of rambling clubs then developed in several major provincial cities. The Manchester Ramblers' Council was set up in 1919, Liverpool and District in 1922, and Sheffield and District Federation in 1926. By the late 1920's, however, many in the outdoor movement began to push harder for the establishment of a national body to represent the interests of ramblers.

As a result the 'Hope Conference' or 'Ramblers Parliament' was organised. This historic meeting was held at Hope, Derbyshire, on October 30th 1927. It was a unique event, for it was the first occasion at which organised ramblers had met on a national basis for national purposes. Delegates were present from many places, including London, Liverpool, Manchester, Leeds and Stockport. They discussed the following issues:

(1)   Footpaths and Rights-of-Way
(2)   The Access to Mountains Bill
(3)   Scenery Preservation
(4)   Preservation of Birds and Wild Flowers
(5)   Railway facilities for Ramblers
(6)   Enclosure of Roadside Wastes
(7)   The Anti-Litter Movement
(8)   National Handbook for Ramblers

Col. Crook, the president of the Peak District and Northern Counties Footpaths Preservation Society was in the chair. He stated that the general public did not realise the extent to which their rights and privileges were being deliberately ignored by landowners. Those present devoted special attention to the pending Access to Mountains Bill, and the Public Rights of Way Bill. The meeting then adopted a resolution calling upon the Government to grant facilities for the passing of the Access to Mountains Bill during the present session. The desirability of forming a National Federation was discussed, and it was resolved to hold an annual conference of federated and kindred societies. (1)

The conferences continued, then an interesting development took place on 31st July 1931 when Nora Willington, General Secretary of The Ramblers' Federation, Manchester and District, wrote to George Mitchell, who was involved in organising the next National Conference, that they wished to place the following resolution before the Council:

"The Manchester & District Ramblers' Federation propose the formation of two Unions – A Union of Northern Ramblers' Federations and Southern Ramblers' Federations – with a joint consultative and co-ordinating Council for consultative and advisory purposes only, such Council to be formed of one delegate from each Federation." (2)

171

However, prior to this, at the conference held at Leicester in October 1928 under the auspices of the National Trust, Scapa, the Commons Society, the Council for the Preservation of Rural England, the Federation of Rambling Clubs, the Peak and Northern Counties Footpaths Preservation Society, and the Leicestershire Footpath Association. (3) R.A. Glen of the Commons Society, an eminent authority on highway law, was billed to speak on "The Rights of Way and Access to Mountains Bill" but failed to do so, because he felt it very "unwise" to deal with such a controversial issue at the conference! It was from this and other experiences with the out-of-doors 'establishment' of the period that the northern ramblers learnt that they were not likely to receive much support from existing amenity organisations for an access to mountains campaign.

T.A. Leonard and George Mitchell subsequently suggested that Manchester was wary of too much power going to London, if and when a national organisation was set up. The issue was discussed again at the Longshaw Conference held on 26th and 27th September 1931, but nothing was resolved. The upshot of all this was that when the Council decided to become the Ramblers' Association in 1935, Manchester decided not to join. However, they finally agreed to "join the fold" in December 1939, just after the outbreak of the 2nd World War. (4)

In the meantime, however, ramblers in many other parts of Britain began to follow the example of the aforementioned 'Areas' by setting up Federations to cover their local counties or cities. According to Tom Stephenson, the sequence was as follows: "In 1930 Federations were in existence in Birmingham, the West Riding of Yorkshire, Nottinghamshire and Derbyshire, Lincolnshire, and north-east Lancashire. A Cumberland Federation was formed in 1932 and changed its name to the Lake District Federation in 1933.* A West of England Federation was also founded in 1932, South Wales in 1933 and the East Riding of Yorkshire in 1938." (5)

*The establishment of The Lake District Federation is particularly interesting for it covers an area which attracts millions of walkers, few of whom actually live in the area. The establishment actually took place at an open-air rally held near Lamplugh, on 17th April 1932. Over 200 people were present. The main speakers were Cyril Farmer and Kenneth Spence. It was formed as the Cumberland Ramblers' Federation, intended to cover just the county of Cumberland, however, at the National Council held at Ilkley the following year, uncertainty arose as to whether Manchester or Liverpool Federations covered Southern Lakeland.

Accordingly, George Mitchell, leading light in the movement, asked them if they would extend this 'Area' to cover all the Lake District, and the name was then changed to the Cumberland and Lake District Federation. In 1933 they published their first 'Lakeland Rambler'. This brought in many members from all parts of England who spent their holidays in the Lake District, so that eventually about a third of their members resided in other areas. (6)

In 1932, the conflict between Manchester ramblers and landowners over access to grouse moors near the city led to the celebrated 'Mass Trespass' on Kinder Scout. Several ramblers were arrested, tried, then imprisoned. However, as this issue will be dealt with in detail in the next chapter it is sufficient to state here that The National Council of Ramblers' Federations did not endorse the event!

In 1934 the decision was taken to convert the National Council of Ramblers' Federations into the Ramblers Association. Accordingly, on 1st January 1935 the Ramblers' Association was officially founded. In the first year of its existence the RA had almost 1,200 individual members and over 300 affiliated rambling clubs. The first piece of legislation that the RA became actively involved in was the seriously flawed Access to Mountains Bill

(1939). Inevitably, the Ramblers soon ended up opposing this maliciously contrived Bill due to amendments and clauses which actually limited access and penalised supposed trespassers! Notwithstanding this the Bill became an Act, although it was never used and was, thankfully, repealed in a later Act. (7) The newly-established RA subsequently became involved in the long campaign to Establish National Parks.

The RA's first office was established at 71 Lord Street, Liverpool in 1938. Soon after this, of course, the 2nd World War broke out, during which traumatic period the RA remained as active as ever. From an Association document of the time entitled 'Enjoyment of the Countryside in Wartime', A Manifesto from the Ramblers' Association we read:

"It will be in the national interest that those citizens who can do so should get into the countryside at regular intervals. There is nothing so beneficial to health, nerves and general well being as a good walk in the country, especially to people who live in towns and those whose work imposes a great strain on them. The Ramblers' Association therefore hopes that every effort will be made by Government and Local Authorities, and by owners and occupiers of land, to maintain rights of way and to provide reasonable freedom to roam over uncultivated land."

In a similar document entitled "Walking in Wartime – Advice from the Ramblers' Association', dated June, 1940, those concerned now clearly felt obliged to add a few words of caution to members intending to walk in the Countryside:

"During the War, and especially if the present anxiety about parachutists and 'Fifth Columnists' continues, it is inevitable that persons walking in the countryside for health and exercise will from time to time be stopped and questioned by the police or the military. It is quite understandable that in present circumstances strangers walking in the countryside and carrying maps, and perhaps cameras, may arouse suspicion. The advice of the Ramblers' Association to people who derive health and pleasure from country walks is – don't give up this best of all pastimes but act with discretion and always carry with you the fullest possible means of identification." (8)

In 1945 the Ramblers' Association moved their office from Liverpool to London. Three years later, in 1948, Tom Stephenson became the RA's first full-time secretary, although it did not become a salaried position until 1952. He was a tireless campaigner for ramblers' rights, and personally organised well-publicised treks in the Pennines for influential MPs. Finally, in 1965, 30 years after Tom Stephenson first suggested the idea, the 250 mile long Pennine Way became the country's first official long-distance footpath. (9) As Stephenson was central to the rambling scene during the 1st part of the 20th century, albeit as a journalist, not a group walker, the early part of his career deserves an appropriate mention at this point.

Tom Stephenson (1893-1987) was born on 12th February 1893 in Chorley, Lancashire. His Father was an engraver in a calico printing works, his mother and grandmother were four-loom weavers in a local cotton mill. When he was fifteen years old he started a seven-year apprenticeship as a block printer. During this period there were frequent periods of short-time working, which left him with spare time to ramble in the nearby hills. It was, in fact, these walks which led him to become a journalist. From 1910 onwards he began to publish accounts of these treks, for which he earned the occasional guinea. (10) One such article appeared in 'Health and Efficiency' in the spring of 1911. Capturing the flavour of the period, in part it read:

"HURRAH! The happy months have come. The trees are clad in radiant hues. The birds are singing from morn till night. Bees are busy amongst the flowers. Butterflies are flitting to and

175

fro. Hedgerows are wreathed in blossom, and the whole countryside seems to teem with life...." (11)

His apprenticeship ended in March 1915. The 1st World War was in full sway, and conscription was in the offing. Out of socialist conviction he registered as a conscientious objector. Inevitably, this led to him being brought before a military tribunal where, to his surprise, he was granted absolute exemption. In 1917 the exemption was cancelled. He was arrested, court-martialled and sentenced to twelve months hard labour. Later in life he was always quick to declare that he would do the same thing again, although he had to concede, when recalling the reaction of his parents, "I think my father was ashamed of me. My mother wept". (12)

In the autumn of 1919 he returned to his old trade of block printing, but this time near London, far away from the northern fells that he loved. (13) It was, however, also in this year – according to Elizabeth Coxhead – that a speech by Phillip Snowden "fired his political zeal" to the extent that for some years he became a keen worker in the Independent Labour Party. (14)

In 1922, when still serving as Labour Party Agent for Dartford, he applied for a job in the Labour Party Research Department, but was just beaten by Barbara Wootton, who subsequently became Lady Wootton, Chairman of the Countryside Commission. Nevertheless, all was not lost, for soon after this he was asked to take charge of the Party's Directory Department, a job in which he was to serve for eleven years. (15) During this period Tom Stephenson rambled all over southern England, but at the same time his thoughts were never far from the north.

In 1933 Stephenson turned to full-time writing, firstly as the editor of *Hiker and Camper,* then as 'Open-Air' correspondent for the *Daily Herald.* Under the heading of "Afoot in Britain" the editor gave Stephenson considerable independence to write radical articles, the most significant of which were about the 'Right to Roam'.

It was during this period – specifically, early in 1935 – that he received a letter from two American girls asking advice about a 'Tramping Tour' in England. In their letter the girls also mentioned their acquaintance with the Appalachian Trail, which runs for 2,000 miles through the Eastern States from Maine to Georgia. Assuming there would be a similar, but smaller trail in Britain, they asked Stephenson if he could recommend such a long-distance walk in Britain. This, of course, he was unable to do, for at this point in time, he was ashamed to admit, none existed! (16)

But the thought that one *should* exist was now firmly planted in Stephenson's mind. In a long article in the *Daily Herald* in June, 1935, he called for the creation of one. He opened by mentioning his correspondence with the Americans then went on to outline in detail a route which he felt should run from the Peaks to the Cheviots:

"By Ashop Head and thence to Bleaklow, across Longdendale and by the Laddow Rocks and Black Chew Head." After crossing the Saddleworth Moors, and Blackstone Edge, in his mind's eye, he saw it continuing north, over Penyghent and then via the Packhorse Trail into Wensleydale, and from thence onwards "over the seemingly endless moors to the crest of Cross Fell, the Pennines topmost height". Then, after more details of his proposed route, he concluded in fine style: "Finally, over bog and moor they would reach the great heaving swells and deep-set glens of the Cheviots". (17)

Tom Stephenson received support for this project from the newly established Ramblers' Association, but to turn the dream into reality required the dedicated labour of many people over a very long period of time. Accordingly, the formal establishment of the

Pennine Way Association took place at Birchfield Guest House, Hope on 26th and 27th February 1938. Representatives of fourteen organisations attended. (18) At this meeting Tom Stephenson outlined his ambitious plan to create a right of way 250 miles long, and also advised them that 68 miles of the proposed trail were not covered by existing rights of way.

It was, in fact, to take another eleven years before an Act was passed making long-distance trails possible! The provision required being in the National Parks and Countryside Act, 1949. Unfortunately, the problems related to getting this trail fully operational, over its entire length, until it was formally opened in 1965, were staggering. Writing as late as 1954 the Sheffield Ramblers noted – once more – that work on the path was held up, chiefly because certain landowners were objecting to the route, or indeed any route, which they felt they could block by legal action. (19)

(L-R) Tom Stephenson, Barbara Castle, Mike Harding and Dr. Arthur Raistrick on Malham Ling, on the Pennine Way Council's occasion to celebrate the 50th anniversary of the opening of the Pennine Way.

Whilst it clearly goes beyond the scope of this short illustrated history of pioneer ramblers to outline in greater detail the struggle to establish this famous long-distance trail, or give much attention to the second part of Tom Stephenson's long and distinguished career, the following should be recorded here:

On the opening of the Pennine Way in 1965: "We came from far and near, by car and coach, train and bus, on cycle and afoot. Councillors and clerks, parliamentarians – ministerial and secretarial – commissioners and colonels, parsons and police, old friends and new, the very aged and the very young, cyclists and walkers, deerstalkers and bonnets, the lords and the commoners, some 2,000 of us, to the untamed, sunny but windswept moorlands above Malham Cove. We came, surely not just to celebrate the opening of the Pennine Way, but to pay tribute to that lad of 13 who, perchance to gaze some 59 years ago from the top of Pendle Hill, saw the glory of the eternal heights, and who since has never deviated from his firm belief that these were for man to tread and find peace and solitude, comfort and friendliness". (20)

On Tom Stephenson: In the spring of 1969, Tom Stephenson withdrew from the Secretaryship of the Ramblers' Association. The decision was his, not the Executive Committee's. In December, 1986, he was conferred with the Honorary Degree of Doctor of Laws at Lancaster University. Sadly, however, just a few months later, on 5th March, 1987, news reached his home town of Chorley that he had died at the age of 94 in Stoke Mandeville Hospital. (21)

THE PENNINE WAY, 1935-1985

A scene from the Pennine Way
Top Withens in Bronte Country, West Yorkshire (Photo: Tom
Stephenson Collection)

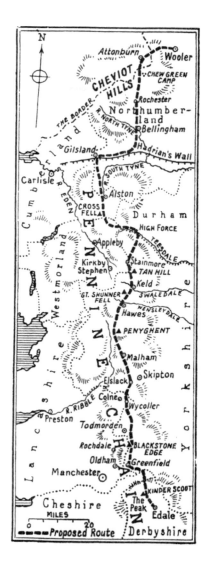

This map of the proposed Pennine Way was prepared by Tom Stephenson and others in 1938. The route today follows a similar line, although in the north it now ends at Kirk Yetholm.

181

CHAPTER FIFTEEN
KINDER SCOUT AND OTHER ACCESS RALLIES

The dramatic event that shook the Ramblers' Federations in the 1930's was the celebrated Kinder Scout Mass Trespass of 1932. Keeping strictly within the law the 'Rambling Establishment' had tried, and tried again, to gain open access to mountain and moorland. Unfortunately, they were still no nearer their goal in 1932 than was James Bryce, back in February 1884. What to do next was the crucial question!

It was a young unemployed motor mechanic from Manchester, Bernard Rothman, with his colleagues in the left-of-centre British Workers Sports Federation who came up with the radical answer. An 'answer' which clearly struck a cord with many rank-and file working class ramblers, but failed to amuse, let alone gain the support of the more staid and conservatively minded leaders of the mainstream Federations. It was, in short, a proposal to organise an illegal mass trespass on Kinder Scout.

Veteran rambler Benny Rothman, age 79, at an RA Access Rally at
Holm village in the Peak, 1990

One of the first reports to be published about the proposed event appeared in the *Manchester Evening News* in mid April 1932. Under an impressively long headline – "Claims to Free Access – Campaign to Force Landowners – Call to Rally – Sunday's Attack on Kinder" – the message was spelt out clearly:

"Tired of unproductive protests and pleas, working class rambling clubs in Lancashire have decided upon direct action to enforce their claims for access to beauty spots in the countryside"

The article then went on to explain that it was the intention of the ramblers to throw 200 or 300 "Shock Troops" into an "Attack" upon Kinder. These new methods, the reporter continued, have been devised by the Lancashire District of the British Workers Sports Federation, and that their affiliated clubs had all been asked to join in the protest. Clubs that were not affiliated, but in sympathy with the aims of the B.W.S.F. were also urged to join the Rally at Hayfield, from which village the 'advance' on Kinder was to be launched on Sunday. Benny Rothman, Secretary of the Lancashire District of this radical Federation then outlined his plans:

"We have fifteen clubs in Lancashire, all of whom will be represented at the rally, which will also be attended by two of our Sheffield clubs." After making remarks about the closing of footpaths in the Kinder area Benny – who was being quoted directly – concluded with these memorable words:

"No doubt we shall find doughty opposition to our advance from gamekeepers and police, but we believe that with sufficient support we can make our action effective. **Ours is a grouse against grouse.** We are willing no longer to be deprived of the beauties of the country for the convenience of the landowners. It is our declared intention to trespass en masse everywhere where we can claim with justice to have a right to go". (1)

183

Grouse driving in Derbyshire

It is, of course, not remarkable that Benny Rothman was able to launch such a radical appeal, for in 1932 unemployment was rife throughout Great Britain, but particularly so in the industrial areas of the north. Living conditions, for the employed and unemployed, were scandalously bad in the grim back streets of cities such as Manchester and Sheffield. The only escape for many working-class people therefore was to make for the countryside whenever they could, the jealously guarded grouse moors of the Peak District and, in particular, the Kinder Scout Plateau, acting as a magnet to such under-privileged workers.

On Sunday 24th April 1932 the weather was fine. The great day had arrived, and large numbers of ramblers – responding to a well-organised leafleting campaign – began to assemble in the picturesque village of Hayfield, which nestles in the Peak, near Kinder Scout. It was from here that the sombre mass of the Kinder Plateau – one of Britains most sacred grouse moors – was to be 'attacked' by Benny Rothman and his B.W.S.F. colleagues.

Throughout the preceding week the local Ramblers' Federation had, of course, done all that was humanly possible to distance themselves from the pending 'Attack' on Kinder. In like manner, the villagers of Hayfield had also done all that was humanely possible to ensure that the radical ramblers were met with as much hostility and obstruction as they could possibly organise.

The advertised plan was for ramblers to meet on the Hayfield Recreation Ground at 2 p.m. Forewarned and forearmed, the Hayfield Parish Council, had taken careful action to stop this happening. By now things were going slightly 'pear-shaped' but still the ramblers kept arriving in the village. Ramblers, of course, were not the only ones to arrive in Hayfield on that fateful day! Predictably, large numbers of Derbyshire police had been called in, armed with special new copies of the bye-laws, one of which, most conveniently, prohibited such meetings on the Recreation Ground. No doubt with great delight, the villagers watched as these were promptly posted in the Recreation Ground.

"The Deputy Chief Constable of Derbyshire and Superintendents McDonald and Else came to see that this regulation was observed, and Mr. Herbert Bradshaw, the Clerk to the Parish Council, was there to read the by-law publicly if the ramblers attempted to make speeches." (2)

Wisely, Benny Rothman and his fellow organisers decided not to play into their hands. Promptly at 2 p.m. the 400–600 strong band of ramblers moved off, taking the lane out of the village which led to Kinder Reservoir and Kinder Scout. Hayfield residents had never seen anything like it before and, I have no doubt, have not done so since! To the clatter of perhaps a thousand hob-nailed boots the Manchester Ramblers passed dramatically through the village, singing the "Red Flag" the "International" and other revolutionary songs as they headed for the hills. (3)

185

The Police, according to Benny Rothman, were caught on the hop. They could not get in front of the ramblers to stop them, or make good use of their vehicles due to the nature of the road. So, on they marched until they reached the first alternative meeting place. Unfortunately, they were immediately advised that they were on Stockport Waterworks land. They moved on until they reached a quarry site, where the acoustics were far better. Benny scrambled onto a ledge and addressed the crowd below. He began by outlining the history of the area, spoke of the injustices of the enclosures, sketched the history of the 'Access to Mountains' campaign, and concluded by giving 'combat' instructions to his colleagues. For example, one blast on the whistle meant stop, two meant turn right, and three for advance in open formation. (4)

The plaque near Hayfield marking the starting point of the 1932 Mass Trespass

The singing protesters marched onwards and upwards, until they got to Nab Brow. At this point they spotted a small group of gamekeepers dotted about on the slopes below Sandy Heys – on the far side of William Clough. A few moments later a well-organised "Advance Guard" dropped down to the stream then started to climb up the other side towards the keepers. At the point where the slope became exceptionally steep they met the keepers. There was a brief discussion, after which a fight started.

The keepers were armed with heavy sticks, which they used enthusiastically to beat the ramblers, however, they were seriously outnumbered, and soon disarmed. In the main, the ramblers just used their hands in this memorable scuffle, but two keepers had their sticks taken from them, which were then used against them! Several other ramblers took their belts off and used them. One spectator was, unfortunately, hit by a small stone, but no one was seriously hurt, apart from one keeper, Mr Edward Beaver, who hurt himself when he lost his balance, rolled down a slope, and twisted his ankle.

After the fight the police chiefs, who had accompanied the mass trespassers, left them alone, to their great though premature relief. The ramblers then turned to the left and continued along the hillside to Ashop Head, the summit of the public footpath from Hayfield to the Snake Inn, then on to the Glossop Sheffield road. Everything then stopped for tea. Whilst thus engaged they were met by about 30 supporters who had come over from Sheffield.

A victory meeting was then held at Ashop Head undisturbed. (Unfortunately, although Ashop Head is, topographically, part of the Kinder Scout massif, it is not on the Kinder Plateau itself, as defined by the Ordnance Survey). A further point of interest is that the victory meeting was actually held on a public path, which does much to explain why they were never actually charged with trespass!) However, leaving aside these troublesome technicalities, speeches were made, and the ramblers then started to make their way back to Hayfield by the usual path down William Clough.

On rejoining the main road the ramblers formed up six abreast and marched towards the village singing and laughing. Alas, this mood was soon to change, for Hayfield was alive with police who were enthusiastically preparing what they considered would be an appropriate welcome for the returning ramblers.

The conclusion of the trespass was particularly bizarre. At the outskirts of the village they were met by a police inspector in what was described as a "baby car." A discussion took place then, at the inspector's suggestion, the ramblers formed up into columns and marched into Hayfield, still over 200 strong, singing triumphantly, the inspector in his "baby car" leading the procession, Pied Piper fashion, into his trap! Surprisingly, these lambs, being led to their own slaughter, still suspected no ill. Their last happy moments came when they were well inside the village. The police stopped them but it was not until officers, accompanied by a keeper began to walk through their ranks that they realised they had been caught. Six men, considered to be the leaders, were taken to the police station and detained. (5)

The lane leading down to the centre of Hayfield where the ramblers were arrested

The ramblers arrested were Bernard Rothman, aged 20, John Anderson, aged 21, Judd Clynes, aged 23, Harry Mendell, aged 23, David Nussbaum, aged 19, and Arthur Gillett, aged 19. They were kept overnight at New Mills. The following day when they all appeared at New Mills Police Court they were charged with unlawful assembly and breach of the peace, and were remanded on bail until 11th May. (6) For reasons mentioned above no charge of trespass was brought against them, for no trespassing had actually occurred. Soon after the great event the Manchester and District Ramblers' Federation made the following declaration:

"Mass Trespass. The Manchester and District Federation wishes to state as definitely as possible, that it had no part in the events which took place in Hayfield and on Kinder Scout on April 24th, and that it had no connection whatsoever with the organisation responsible for the happenings on that day...". (7)

On Monday 25th April Sir Lawrence Chubb also felt moved to register his disapproval of the event. In a letter to George Mitchell, Secretary of the National Council of Ramblers' Federations, he stated that it was his view that the event had been a "peculiarly stupid and mischievous business and those arrested should rightly face the consequences of their own foolhardiness". (8) (One suspects, however, that the factor responsible for generating such a total lack of solidarity from others in the rambling movement was Benny Rothman's politics!

The Trial at Derby Assizes. After three adjournments at the Petty Divisional Court the accused were finally committed to the Assizes at Derby. By which time all the pro-rambling witnesses had been obliged to drop out, as they were poor, and could not afford the fare, expenses, or time off work. The trial was held at Derby on the 7th and 8th of July, where the six youths were tried before a totally 'impartial' jury, in the main composed of high-ranking military officers and country gentlemen! All of whom, in practice, could be

189

totally relied on to be biased against ramblers in general, and socialist ones in particular. (9)

(The accused in court were listed as John Thomas Anderson, 21, a cotton piecer, who, in addition to being charged, along with the rest, with "riotously assembling to disturb the public" was also charged with maliciously inflicting greivous bodily harm on Edward Beever – the keeper who had accidentally hurt his ankle! Also charged were Bernard Rothman, 21, now listed as a storekeeper; Julius Clyne, 23, machinist; Harry Mendel, 22 machinist; Anthony Walter Gillett, 19, student, and David Nussbaum, 19, labourer, all of whom were charged with "Riotous Assembly")

In the prosecution case – and although completely irrelevant – a great deal was made of the fact that on the 'Trespass' there were distinct shouts of "Down with the Landlords and the Ruling Classes" – and – "Up with the Workers". In addition to which many people had actually been heard singing 'The Red Flag". Nussbaum had also been seen brazenly selling a paper called *The Daily Worker* which, it was implied, was clearly some sort of crime, although a difficult one for the prosecution to define in precise legal terms.

Unfortunately, due to serious cash-flow problems, Benny Rothman (in common with most of his co-defendants) elected to defend himself. He addressed the jury at length, and in a very competent manner. The outline of the case he put being fairly summarised by a reporter from *The Derbyshire Advertiser*.

On April 24th, he stated, some 300 ramblers gathered together to protest against the enclosure of certain moors in Derbyshire. Certain sections of moorland were closed to ramblers, who went out at week-ends to enjoy sunshine and a change of scene. The ramblers found that only certain footpaths were open to them, footpaths which were so crowded that ramblers might as well stay at home in the towns. "There is nothing unreasonable in our demands to use uncultivated land in the Peak", declared Rothman. (10)

Benny Rothman then went on to argue that they were not a mob of hooligans, and that if they had gone to the moors with the intention of fighting how was it that only one keeper got hurt when there were so many ramblers? He added, their intentions had been peaceful from the start, for as soon as they were told they could not hold a meeting at Hayfield they had moved away. The object of agreeing on "military signals" and advancing in "open order" had been to avoid trouble.

Nussbaum, who also made his defence from the dock, said he was not a rambler, and did not belong to the British Workers' Sports Federation. He went up to Hayfield to sell the *Daily Worker,* and that was all he did. Anderson, on oath, claimed he had nothing to do with the British Workers' Sports Federation, and that he had gone to Hayfield on 24th April out of curiosity. He also emphatically denied that he had caused Beever's injuries. Gillett, the student, admitted going to Hayfield to carry out a mass trespass. There was no intention of violence, he added, and did not see anyone knocked down.

"General Rothman" Lord Big Bug and Lady Little Flea.
There was, of course, no doubt that this was a political trial, albeit a farcical one. "General Rothman," the jury was solemnly advised by the prosecution, had actually been seen – and by reliable witnesses – leading his "Hikers" back from Kinder Scout singing the "Red Flag." Further to this some present had also been heard shouting "Down with the Landlords and up with the workers" and "Down with the Bobbies". In the perpetration of these heinous crimes the prosecution then made it very clear that they looked upon Rothman not as a "Shining Light" but as a "Leading Light" in the affair, adding, the other five youths were also leaders.

191

Most damning of all, however, was one of the exhibits put in by the prosecution. It was a notice posted in the locality in which the British Workers' Sports Federation had called upon ramblers not to pass pious resolutions on the Access to Mountains Bill, but to take action to prevent mountains and moors being closed to them. One particularly memorable sentence in it read: " Is it a crime for working-class feet to tread on sacred ground on which Lord Big Bug and Lady Little Flea do their shooting."

After a lengthy summing up the sentences were passed down. Mendel was discharged through lack of evidence. Anderson, found guilty of occasioning bodily harm, was sentenced to six months. The rest were found guilty of incitement to cause a riotous assembly. Benny Rothman was sentenced to four months, Nussbaum, presumably for selling the *Daily Worker*, three months, Clyne and Gillett to two months imprisonment. (11)

The Aftermath.   The immediate reaction from the public and the media was that although they expected the participants to be punished the universal opinion was that the sentences were out of all proportion to the crimes. The *Manchester Guardian* made the point that the whole affair had borne a remarkable resemblance to a university rag, when arrested persons were not usually sent to a High Court and given custodial sentences. (12)

After the event, and imprisonment, Benny Rothman rightly claimed that the reaction from individual ramblers, and the public at large, had been very positive. To validate this claim he quoted Frank Turton, a prominent figure in the open-air movement, who stated, soon after the event, that the Trespass had indeed led to a greater awareness of the injustices of the situation and that national interest had been aroused as never before. Rothman also drew attention to the fact that the annual demonstration of ramblers at Winnats Pass, Castleton, on June 26th 1932, had been attended by no less than 10,000 ramblers, a record figure which he attributed to the publicity gained by the Kinder Trespass. (13)

On the other hand, Philip Daley of the Manchester Ramblers' Federation, and later on the RA Executive, claimed that the access subsequently gained in the area owed nothing whatsoever to the Trespass! In fact, writing fifty years after the event, he indicated that he still felt the same way! "I can say quite categorically and without fear of contradiction, that the 'Mass Trespass' on Kinder Scout was a positive hindrance and deterrent to the discussions and negotiations to secure the freedom of the hills." (14)

Tom Stephenson was also far from sympathetic, but he did concede that claims that the Mass Trespass had actually put back any hopes of access for twenty years were nonsense, adding, the Creech Jones Access to Mountains Bill of 1939, had been literally butchered by Parliament. He then went on to state, less than generously, that the best thing, or rather the *only* good thing to stem from the demonstration was Ewan McColl's famous song, 'The Manchester Rambler'. (15)

Abbey Brook. One wonders, however, was it the principle of engaging in 'confrontational' events that Philip Daley and Tom Stephenson were complaining about, or was it the fact that they had been decidedly "Upstaged" by a radical, young working-class lad of 21, from the back streets of Manchester? Alas, and with all due respect to Philip and Tom, I suspect it was the latter! The evidence for this view stems from the fact that the second, now largely forgotten, and decidedly more confrontational mass protest took place at Abbey Brook, on Sunday 18th September, just five months after the Kinder Scout confrontation. The point to note was that this confrontation was organised by the Manchester Ramblers' Federation!

On this particularly challenging occasion a small army of ramblers met with formidable opposition from a large contingent of about a hundred gamekeepers, all well armed with heavy wooden cudgels, and backed up by police officers. All of which is truly amazing, for G.B.H. Ward had researched the issue with great care, and virtually established that the disputed track was a public right of way.

After a minor scuffle the cudgel-wielding keepers appeared to lose all self- control, and began to rain down blows on the heads and shoulders of the ramblers with their heavy weapons. Things then got so bad that the police officer in charge, obviously fearing serious injury, or even death, and a national scandal, advised the keepers to aim for their legs only. What particularly incensed the keepers was that their brutal tactics failed to stop the trespassers from reaching the disputed track. Rather surprisingly, there were no serious injuries and no arrests. (16)

The Keeper's Cottage.

A head keeper in the yard of his substantial cottage. In the demonology of keepers and landowners no time was lost in placing ramblers on the long list of creatures, great and small, they felt appropriate to classify as undesirable vermin.

194

As already indicated, unity of purpose on the whole question of open access to mountains and moorland was being deliberately undermined from within the ranks of the 'Out-of-Doors' movement by Sir Lawrence Chubb, then Secretary of the aforementioned Commons Open Spaces and Footpath Preservation Society. Opposition by Chubb's society, and its kindred organisations, such as the Council for the Preservation of Rural England, first surfaced in 1928, then at an exceptionally broad-based conference held at Leicester in 1929. With delegates from a great many 'Sporting Organisations' present, Chubb, (supposedly) on behalf of the Open Spaces Society made it very clear that they would refuse to associate with the public demands for the public right of access to uncultivated mountain and moorland!

A special one-day conference organised by the Open Spaces and Footpath Preservation Society in October 1931, reversed this stand, when the Society declared for Access, but this in no way inhibited Chubb, who continued to work against this policy! Notwithstanding the corrected position of Chubb's own organisation, in a letter to *The Field,* which was published in June 1932, he declared that the action of the Kinder Scout hikers was indefensible. In another letter to George Mitchell, Secretary of the Ramblers' Federations, written the day after the Kinder Trespass, he condemned it as a stupid, mischievous business. His hard, unsympathetic view was that the youths arrested should rightly face the consequences of their foolish actions. (The fact that his own Society had illegally organised navvies to pull down fences at Berkhamstead, and associates in the 'Sunday Tramps' made a particular point of trespassing on *all* their walks, seems to have been conveniently forgotten by Chubb!)

To compound matters, however, in a particularly memorable speech Chubb made to the Manchester Luncheon Club on 3rd December 1934 he attacked the whole principle of open access to mountain and moorland. This he did by arguing that these demands failed to take into account the fine old English attribute of fair play to both sides. Bearing in mind that Chubb was speaking at a time of mass unemployment, when the side of society represented by Benny Rothman were not receiving an excessive allocation of "fair play" his views on this crucial issue naturally aroused bitter denunciation from many in the rambling movement.

The Sheffield Federation, in particular, was to the fore in protesting against Chubb's pro-establishment line on access. In a satirical article Royce declared "fair play on the Peak – what mocking laughter would echo from the cliffs in the Winnats if that statement was made there". (17) Which, of course, brings us to the great 'Access' rallies that were held at the Winnats Pass in Derbyshire throughout the thirties.

The Winnats Pass Access Rallies. The Winnats Pass Access demonstration held on 1st July 1935 was typical of many held during this decade. Five thousand ramblers, mainly from the great industrial cities and towns of Lancashire gathered at this famous pass to argue the case once more for greater access to uncultivated mountain and moorland. Alderman Fred Marshall, Deputy Mayor of Sheffield presided, and it is fitting that he did, for in 1910 he had been a fully paid up member of the radical Clarion Rambling Club.

In his speech Marshall made the point that the opportunity to enjoy rambling had become more restricted, cars were "monopolising" the lanes and roads used by walkers and, on the footpaths, 'Trespassers will be Prosecuted' signs were far more numerous than they had been 25 years ago. Marshall also reminded ramblers that local authorities had acquired thousands of acres of land, but he regretted to say that gaining access to these moors was proving to be just as difficult as on land held under private ownership.

The famous Dr. Cyril Edwin Murchison Joad, university reader in philosophy, broadcaster, and author of several books on rambling, then moved the resolution calling upon the Government to grant immediate facilities for the passing of the Access to Mountains Bill. He also urged the Manchester, Sheffield, Stockport and Chesterfield Local Authorities, who owned thousands of acres of land in the Peak, to throw them open to the public. This resolution was carried. Joad then went on to make the all-important point that ramblers did not want footpaths over moors, but the right to wander over them where they pleased, which demand, he felt, should be made a political issue at the next election.

After praising *some* of the work of The Council for the Preservation of Rural England, Joad added that that it was, in his opinion, an organisation that was too anxious to stand well with all the important interests concerned. The National Trust, too, which had acquired thousands of acres of land all over the country, did not escape censure by Joad, who went on to advise those present that it was, in his opinion, a compromising body, anxious not to offend anybody!

The next speaker at this great rally was the well-known rambler Phil Barnes who, being an active supporter of the Sheffield and Peak District branch of the Council for the Preservation of Rural England, quite understandably, made no attempt to endorse Joad's reservations about this organisation. Joad and Barnes, albeit in their different ways, played significant roles in the long, ongoing campaign to gain access to mountain and moorland in the 1930's – the former being a national celebrity. The latter was a noted regional activist who, today, is still remembered in the movement as the author of *Trespassers will be Prosecuted,* which he published himself in 1934. Two-thirds of the gross receipts from the sale of this book were subsequently donated to an appeal fund to acquire Surprise View, Hathersage, for the nation. (18)

G.B.H. Ward of Sheffield addressing a Winnats Pass demonstration

The struggle for greater access to the countryside in general, and open access to mountain and moorland in particular had, of course, continued at Parliamentary level throughout the first part of the 20th Century. Annan Bryce tried once more in 1909, but then no further attempts were made with an Access Bill until 1924. Between then and 1938 another nine Bills were introduced, all based, more or less, on the original Bill presented by James Bryce in 1884. Campaigning efforts, however, were crowned with a measure of success in 1925 with the passing of The Law of Property Act, which established a public right of access to common land in urban areas. The most substantial gain from this legislation was that it created a right of access to the central and Southern Lakeland fells, which happened to fall within Windermere Urban District Council.

In 1935, soon after the federations of rambling clubs had united to form the Ramblers' Association, serious, united lobbying began for access to mountains, as well as long distance paths, national parks and measures to better protect all public rights of way. These efforts eventually appeared to be successful when, in 1938, Arthur Creech-Jones obtained a Second Reading for his Access to Mountains Bill. The Bill then became an Act of Parliament, when it was realised that it was highly defective, in fact, positively dangerous, notably because of the infamous clause four, which would, in some circumstances have made harmless trespass a criminal offence! Fortunately, it was never used, and was finally repealed after World War 2 by the National Parks and Access to the Countryside Act 1949. (19)

Meanwhile, during the late 1920's and the 1930's The Ramblers Federations, then the Association, continued to campaign and demonstrate in their respective areas in favour of an 'Access to Mountains Bill'. For example, following on the lines of the Manchester Federation who were already active in this work, the Liverpool and District Ramblers' Federation held their 1st access and public rights of way rally at Thurstaston, on the Wirral, on June 25th 1927. The meeting was addressed by Dr. Ernest Baker, J.H. Hayes MP for Edge Hill and Mr Andrew Blair. (20)

Federation Demonstration, Thurstaston Hill, June 25th 1927

199

The 1928 rally was a more impressive affair, "With the red sandstone of Thor's Stone on Thurstaston Common as a 'backcloth' and the heather-clad slopes of the hill opposite as the auditorium, an ideal setting was formed for Saturday's demonstration by Merseyside ramblers to advance the freer use of Britain's wild places for walkers and mountaineers" (21)

Among the 300 or so people present was the Mayor of Birkenhead, Ald. F. Naylor, Mr Andrew Blair, and Mr. Charles Porter, President of the Federation. The Right Hon. C.P. Trevelyan, Minister of Education in the Labour Government, moved a resolution expressing concern at the number of footpaths which were being lost to the public, and urged the Government to pass two Bills aimed at resolving these problems. Andrew Blair, leading light of the Merseyside Ramblers' Federation, and life-long campaigner for the protection of footpaths then stated that The Rights of Way Bill had been considered by Parliament many times, and thought the time was ripe for the Government to adopt it. (22)

As ramblers are aware, the struggle to obtain access to Britain's mountains and moorland, and preserve our wonderful heritage of public paths continued throughout the remainder of the 20th Century. Then, late in 2000, the Government honoured it's election pledge to extend access to the open countryside when it passed 'The Countryside and Rights of Way Act'.

The Act gives the public the legal right to walk in areas of unimproved, extensively grazed open country, although, at times, land may be 'closed' for a particular reason; for example, when there is a risk of fire, or to protect nesting birds. Putting the new Act into operation, however, will be a long and fairly complicated process. Nevertheless, we remain optimistic, although we all recognise that it still remains to be seen how it will work out in practice.

To many people, however, the right to wander at will on *our* open mountains, and moorlands, and to walk on *our* public rights of way, freed of obstructions, isn't just about enjoying Britain's very beautiful countryside. It is a statement that questions the legitimacy of an almost feudal system of rural land usage. It is a statement about citizenship and democratic rights and, last but not least, it is a statement about defending *our* collective 'Green' heritage for the benefit of all future generations.

Today, more than ever, surely we all need to re-establish a genuine relationship with our island homeland – and each other! Those who live in the towns and cities need to re-discover a spiritual relationship with the countryside, and those who live in the country need to re-examine their own historic links with the majority who now live in our urban areas. In most cases a majority whose immediate ancestors once lived, and worked, in either the Scottish glens, the Welsh valleys, or the English shires, but now, due to historical, social and industrial factors, way beyond their control, are now confined to our cities, towns and suburbs.

Overcoming anti-urban prejudice, backed by an endless variety of propaganda, aimed at keeping the now urbanised majority of British people out of *our* countryside has, of course, been a central feature of campaigns for access to the countryside for decades. To conclude, let us hope this short history of the pioneering days of the rambling movement will help many people, urban and rural, walkers and non-walkers alike, to reach a better understanding of the rambling movement.

"HOW TO MAKE A SOCIALIST."

Knowing he is too poor to go to law—steal his bits of Common and shut him out.

Then stop his footpaths. [From "*Fun*," 28/12/87.

Taken from the right of centre satirical magazine 'Fun'. It was reproduced by Henry Allnut, Secretary to the National Footpaths Preservation Society, who published it in his 'Footpath Manual' c1887. The use of this paternalist item by Allnut provides us with a unique insight into his underlying social and political motivation.

REFERENCES

CHAPTER ONE   THE BATTLE OF GLEN TILT

1   Mackenzie, Alexander. *The History of the Highland Clearances.* First published by Mackenzie, Inverness, 1883. Reprinted by Mercat Press, Perth. 1979 edition. p 340

2   Bateman, John, *The Great Landowners of Great Britain*, Harrison. p 15

3   Gladstone, Hugh S. *Record Bags and Shooting Records.* London, Wetherby, 1930. pp 172 173

4   *The Times.* 15th October, 1850

5   Ibid. 17th October, 1850

6   Ibid. 30th October, 1850

7   *Punch.* Volume of 1850. p 144

8   Stephenson, Tom. RA *Rucksack,* Vol. 10, No. 1. Winter, 1980

9   Mackenzie, Alexander. *The Story of the Highland Clearances.* pp 340, 341

10   Ibid. pp 341-343

11   Ibid. p 347

12   Prebble, John. *The Highland Clearances.* Penguin Books, Harmondsworth, 1969. p 308

13   Mackenzie, Alexander. *The History of the Highland Clearances.* p 119

14   Martineau, Harriet. *Harriet Martineau's Autobiography.* Reprinted by Virago Press, London, 1983. p 139

15   Linklater, Eric. *The Lion and the Unicorn.* George Routledge & Sons, London, 1935. pp 79, 81

CHAPTER TWO   HEADING FOR THE HIGHLANDS

1   *The Illustrated London News.* 19th August, 1871

2   *The Graphic*, 13th September, 1873

3   *The Illustrated London News*, July 30th 1881

4   Linklater, Eric. *The Lion and the Unicorn.* pp 79-80

5   Morrison, the Rev. G.A. In an introduction to Hugh Macdonald's *Rambles Round Glasgow.* John Smith & Son, Glasgow, 1910. pp xx - xxv

6   Ibid. pp xxix – xxxx

7   Ibid. p xlv

8   *The Times*, Monday, 26th December, 1892

9   Hill, Howard, *Freedom to Roam.* Moorland Publishing, Ashbourne, 1980. p 24

10   *The Times*, Monday, 26th December, 1892

CHAPTER THREE   WINANS VERSUS MURDO MACRAE

1   *Report of Her Majesty's Commission of Inquiry into the Condition of the Crofters and Cottars in the Highlands and Islands of Scotland.* (1884). In, *British Parliamentary Papers, Agriculture (Highland Crofters)* Volume 21. Irish University Press Edition. Shannon, Ireland, 1969 (Intro.) (Thereinafter – BPP. IUP.)

2   Ibid. p 84

3   Ibid. p 90

4   Ibid. p 94

5   Ibid. 'Appendix C' *List of Deer Forests in Scotland.* (1883) p 532

6   Ibid. Appendix' A p 491

7   *Dictionary of American Biography.* Humprey Milford, Oxford University Press, and Charles Scribners' Sons, New York. Vol. XX p 371-373

8   Ibid.

9   *Calendar of Probate.* Volume U-Z, 1897. p 190

10   Mackay, I.R. *The Pet Lamb Case.* In, *The Transactions of the Gaelic Society of Inverness.* Volume 48 (1972-74) p 189.

11   BPP. IUP. Volume 25. p 237

12   Ibid. p 243

13   BPP. IUP. Volume 24. pp 220

14   Mackay I.R. *The Pet Lamb Case.* p 193-194

15   BPP. IUP. Volume 25 p 242

16   *The Times*, 21st October 1885

17   Mackay I.R. *The Pet Lamb Case.* p 198

18   Ibid.

19   *Calendar of Probate*, 1878

20   *Calendar of Probate,* 1897

21   McConnochie, Alexander Inkson. *The Deer Forests of Scotland; Descriptive, Sporting.* H.F. & G. Witherby, London, 1923. p 48

22   BPP. IUP. Volume 21, "Appendix C." p 532

23   McConnochie, *The Deer Forests of Scotland.* p 49

CHAPTER FOUR   JAMES BRYCE AND THE ACCESS BILLS

1   The Dictionary of National Biography, 1922 –1930. ('B') Oxford University Press. pp 127 –128

2   The Cairngorm Club Journal, 1896

3   The Times, January 23rd 1922

4   Fisher, H.A.L. James Bryce (Viscount Bryce of Dechmont, O.M.) Macmillan & Co. London 1927, Vol. 1. p 280-281

5   BPP. *Access to Mountains (Scotland) Bill.* Volume 1 1884. p 90-91

6   *The Times.* 25th March 1884
7   BPP. *Mountains, Rivers and Pathways (Wales) Bill 1888.* p 129
8   *Parliamentary Debates.* Fourth Series: Victoria, 1892. Vol. 11
        Second volume of the Session. (*Access to Mountains (Scotland) Bill.*pp
        93-94
9   Baker, Ernest A. *The Forbidden Land etc.* London, 1924. p 4
10   BPP. *Access to Mountains (Scotland) Bill.* (71) 14th February, 1898
11   *The Times,* 14th May 1924
12   Fisher, H.A.L. *James Bryce.* Vol. 1. pp 282 –283

CHAPTER FIVE   THE COMMONS AND OPEN SPACES SOCIETY

1   *The Dictionary of National Biography.* 1922-1930. Oxford University
        Press, 1937.   pp 764-767
2   Ibid.
3   Ashbrook, Kate. *The Open Spaces Society.* An essay on the history of
        the Society. p 1
4   Hill, Howard, *Freedom to Roam.* Moorland Publishing, 1980. p 20
5   *The Dictionary of National Biography.* 1912-1921. Oxford University
        Press, 1927.   pp 278-279
6   Stephenson, Tom. *Forbidden Land – The Struggle for Access to
        .Mountain and Moorland.* Manchester University Press, 1989. p 142
7   *The Times,* 19th February, 1948
8   *The Illustrated London News.* 19th June 1869
9   Hill, William Thompson. *Octavia Hill – Pioneer of the National Trust
        and Housing Reform, by Her Kinsman.* Hutchinson, London, 1956. p 126

10   Eversley, Lord. *Commons, Forests and Footpaths.* Cassell & Company,
        London, 1910. p 19
11   *The Illustrated London News.*11th October 1879
12   Simpson, A.L. *The Work of the Commons, Open Spaces and Footpath
        Preservation Society during 1932.* In, *The Ramblers Yearbook for 1933.*
        [The Liverpool and District Ramblers' Federation 1933.]

CHAPTER SIX THE SUNDAY TRAMPS

1   *The Dictionary of National Biography.* Oxford University Press,
        London, Humprey Milford, 1920. Supplement, January 1901-1911 pp
        398-405
2   Ibid.
3   Maitland, Frederick William, *The Life and Letters of Leslie Stephen.*
        Duckworth & Company, London. MCMVI. p 358

4   *The Atlantic Monthly,* 1905. Vol. 95. p 351
5   *The Times,* 18th January, 1930
6   *The Atlantic Monthly,* 1905. Vol. 95. p 252
7   Maitland, F.W. *The Life and Letters of Leslie Stephen.* pp 358, 359
8   Annan, Noel Gilroy, *Leslie Stephen his Thought and Character in Relation to his Time.* Macgibbon & Kee, London, 1951. p. 89
9   *The Times,* 30th January, 1930
10   *The Dictionary of National Biography.* 1901-1911. 1922-1930.
11   Ibid. 1901-1911 (Supplement) Vol. 1. pp. 656, 657
12   Smythe, F.S. *Edward Whymper.* Hodder & Stourton, pp. 318, 319

CHAPTER SEVEN   PIONEER RAMBLING CLUBS 1874 - 1900

1   Hollett, David. *Passage to the New World.* P.M. Heaton Publishing, Abergavenny, 1995. pp 63, 64
2   Fordham, Montague. *The English Agricultural Labourer 1300-1925.* The Labour Publishing Company, London, 1925. p 53
3   *The Illustrated London News.* January 28th 1888. p 80
4   *The Dictionary of National Biography.* Supplement, January 1901. December 1911. Vol. 1. Oxford University Press, London. pp 674, 675
5   *The New Standard Encyclopaedia.* Odhams Press, London, 1923. p 1299
6   Allen, F.A. (General Secretary, Y.M.C.A., Liverpool, and Chairman of Ramblers' Federation, 1927). In, *The Ramblers' Handbook for 1927.* pp 35,36
7   Hill, Howard. *Freedom to Roam.* Moorland Publishing, 1980. p 21
8   *Forest Ramblers' Journal,* 1886
9   *The Gipsy Journal and British Tourist.* April 1896. p 123
10   *The Graphic.* 18th September 1886
11   *The Yorkshire Ramblers' Club Journal.* 1901-1902. p 4
12   Ibid. p xii
13   Ibid. p. 9
14   Ibid. 1903-1908. p 170
15   Ibid. 1910. pp 198-203.
16   Ibid. p 197
17   Ibid. 1912-1921. pp 251-258
18   Ibid. p 257

CHAPTER EIGHT   THE SHEFFIELD CLARION RAMBLERS

1   Hill, Howard, *Freedom to Roam etc.* p 31
2   *The Dictionary of National Biography,* 1941-1950. Oxford University
       Press, 1959. p 96
3   *The Dictionary of National Biography,* 1971-1980 Oxford University
       Press 1986.
4   Stephenson, Tom. *Forbidden Land etc.* p 80
5   *The Times,* 12th March 1907
6   *The North Wales Times,* 14th March 1903
7   *Sheffield Clarion Ramblers' Handbook,* 1948-1949. p 3
8   Ibid
9   Ibid. pp 9 -12

CHAPTER NINE   LONG DISTANCE WALKING

1   Murray, Geoffrey, *The Gentle Art of Walking,* Blackie & Sons Ltd.,
       London, 1939. pp 30.31. Citing - *The Life of Foster Powell.* (Pamphlet)
2   *The Manchester Guardian,* Friday 5th May 1903
3   Ibid.
4   *The Illustrated London News* (Supplement) October 6th 1877. p 338
5   *The Illustrated London News* (Supplement) November 9th 1878. p 445
6   *The Graphic,* March 15th 1884. p 256. (Citing the *Daily Telegraph*)
7   *The Manchester Guardian.* May 13th 1903
8   Ibid.
9   Murray, Geoffrey. *The Gentler Art of Walking.* p 27. (Citing Thom.
       Walter - *Pedestrianism,* and Baddely, *The English Lake District.*)
10   Smith, Brian, *Long Distance Walkers Association – A Brief History*
              (Letter to the author 20th October 1998)
11   Ibid.

CHAPTER TEN   THE LAKE DISTRICT AND THE 'LAKERS'

1   West, T.A. *A Guide to the Lakes in Cumberland, Westmorland and
       Lancashire.* London, 1778
2   Marchant, W.M. In an introduction to: *A Guide through the District of
       the Lakes* by William Wordsworth. Ruper Hart-Davis. London, 1951. p
       19
3   Ibid. p 13
4   Brinton, Crane, *The Political Ideas of the English Romanticists.* Oxford
       University Press (Humphey Milford) London, 1926. p 48

5   Stephenson, *In Praise of Walking Tours* – In *The Manchester City News* 23rd August 1902.
6   *Dictionary of National Biography. Smith, Elder & Co.,* London, 1900 Vol. LX111. pp 12,13
7   Ibid. p 14
8   *The Westmorland Gazette and Kendal Advertiser,* 24th April, 1847
9   *Dictionary of National Biography,* Smith, Elder & Co., London, 1893. Vol. XXXV1. pp 311-313
10   Martinaeu, Harriet. *Biographical Sketches,* Macmillan & Co., London, 1870. p 404
11   *The Graphic* 27th January, 1900
12   *Dictionary of National Biography,*1912 –1921. Oxford University Press, 1927, p 258
13   *Punch or London Charivari.* 5th February, 1876
14   *The Manchester Guardian* 7th October, 1887.
15   Ibid.
16   *The Illustrated London News,* 7th July, 1860.

CHAPTER ELEVEN
SOME EARLY 20th CENTURY RAMBLING CLUBS

1   *The Rucksack Club Journal,* 1923. Vol.V.No. 1 p 1
2   *Manchester City News* 23rd August 1902
3   Ibid. 30th August 1902
4   Ibid. 20th September 1902
5   *The Rucksack Club Journal* 1923 pp 5,6.
6   Ibid. pp 14,15
7   Ibid. Vol. 1V. 1912-1922. p 248
8   *The Manchester Guardian* – mid May 1904
9   Murray, Geoffrey, *The Gentle Art of Walking.* Blackie & Sons, London & Glasgow, 1939 p 230
10   *The Ramblers Handbook, 1915.* pp 40,88
11   *The Graphic* August 27th 1887
12   *The Ramblers' Handbook, 1915.* pp 87-94
13   Ibid. 1914   pp 43, 44
14   Ibid. p 45
15   Ibid. pp 98,99
16   *The Ramblers' Handbook,1927. The Official Year-Book of the Liverpool and District Ramblers' Federation.* pp 17-23

CHAPTER TWELVE   THE NINETEEN THIRTIES

1   *Who was Who, 1951-1960.* Adam & Charles Black, London. Vol 5. p 587
2   Joad, C.E.M. *A Charter for Ramblers.* In *The Ramblers' Yearbook, 1932.* p 55
3   Joad, C.E.M. *The Horrors of the Countryside.* Leonard and Virginia Wolff at the Hogarth Press, London, 1931
4   Graham, Stephen. *The Gentle Art of Tramping.* Robert Holden & Co., London, 1927. pp 1-7
5   *The Manchester Evening Chronicle,* 29th April 1932
6   *The Times,* 8th October 1934
7   *The Y.H.A. Rucksack,* Autumn 1936, Vol.4 No. 4. p 81
8   *The Ramblers' Yearbook* 1934
9   Ibid. 1927
10   Ibid. 1932
11   Ibid. 1927
12   Ibid. 1928
13   Ibid. 1932
14   Leonard, T. Arthur. *Adventures in Holiday Making etc.* The Holiday Fellowship, London. 1934 p 19
15   Ibid. p 53
16   *The Ramblers' Yearbook for 1930.* p 29
17   Ibid. 1934. p 15

CHAPTER THIRTEEN THE YOUTH HOSTEL ASSOCIATION

1   Joad, C.E.M. *A Charter for Ramblers, or The Future of the Countryside.* Hutchinson & Co. Ltd., London, 1933. p 15
2   Coburn, Oliver. *Youth Hostel Story.* The National Council of Social Service, London, 1950. p 8
3   Otten, Karl. *A Combine of Aggression – Masses, Elite, and Dictatorship in Germany.* George Allen & Unwin Ltd., London 1942.   p 74
4   Ibid. p 76
5   Butler, Rohan. *The Roots of National Socialism.* Faber & Faber, London 1941. p 51
6   Otto, Dr. Heinrich. *The German Youth Movement Before and After the War.* In, *The Friends Quarterly Examiner* (The Society of Friends) British Periodicals Ltd., London & Philadelphia P.A. 1935. p 167
7   Ibid. p 169

8   Cole, J.A. *Just Back from Germany.* Faber & Faber, London 1931. p 97

9   Coburn Oliver. *Youth Hostel Story.* pp 16, 17

10   *Liverpool Daily Post and Mercury.* 30th September 1929

11   *The Ramblers' Yearbook 1929.* p 13

12   *The Ramblers' Yearbook* 1931. p 25

13   Ibid. 1932. p 26

14   *The Times.* 3rd & 28th November 1936

15   Baron, Barclay. *The First Ten Years of The Y.H.A.* In *Rucksack,* Autumn 1940. p. 74,77

16   *The Ramblers' Association Annual Report and Accounts, 1997.* p 29

CHAPTER FOURTEEN   THE RAMBLERS ASSOCIATION

1   *The Ramblers' Yearbook for 1928.* pp 78,79

2   Wilmington to Mitchell, 31st July 1931. (RA archive material "Tom Stephenson Box, London Metropolitan Archives

3   Stephenson, Tom. *Forbidden Land.* Manchester University Press, © Ramblers' Association 1989. p 81,82

4   Ibid. pp 84, 85.

5   Ibid. p. 81

6   Rowland to Tom, July 28th 1977. (RA archive material 'Tom Stephenson Box' London Metropolitan Archives

7   *A Short Guide to the Ramblers' Association* (*RA Fact Sheet No.4*) p 3

8   *Walking in Wartime* – RA Advice Sheet, Liverpool, June 1940

9   *RA Fact Sheet No. 4.* p 5

10   Stephenson, Tom. *The Way I Have Come.* In, *The Countryman* Spring 1969. pp. 51- 65

11   Stephenson, T.C. *The Call of the Country: the Things You May Find on a Ramble.* In, *Health and Strength* 20th May 1911. p 496

12   *Countryside Commission News* May-June 1985

13   Stephenson, Tom. *The Way I have Come* (Part 2) In, *The Countryman* Summer 1962. p 238

14   Coxhead, Elizabeth. *Tom Stephenson: a Portrait.* In, *Ramblers' News* Spring, 1950. p. 4

15   RA *Rucksack.* Spring, 1969

16   *Readers Digest.* April 1974. p 173

17   Stephenson, Tom. *Wanted, a Long Green Trail"* In, *The Daily Herald* 22 June 1935.

18   *Sheffield Clarion Ramblers' Handbook.* 1954, pp 69.70

19   Ibid.

20   RA *Rucksack.* Spring, 1965

21   *The Chorley Guardian,* 5th March 1987

CHAPTER FIFTEEN
KINDER SCOUT AND OTHER ACCESS RALLIES

1   *The Manchester Evening News,* 18th April 1932
2   *The Manchester Guardian,* 25th April 1932
3   Ibid.
4   Rothman, Benny. *The 1932 Kinder Trespass.* Willow Publishing,
    Altringham,
    1980 p 24
5   *The Manchester Guardian,* 26th April, 1932
6   *The Evening Chronicle,* 26th April 1982
7   *The Signpost* (Bulletin of the Manchester & District Ramblers'
    Federation) Supplement, May 1932
8   Stephenson, Tom, *Forbidden Land.* Manchester University Press, 1989,
    p 162
9   *The Progressive Rambler,* April 1942
10   *The Derbyshire Advertiser,* 8th July 1932
11   Ibid
12   *The Manchester Guardian,* 11th July 1932
13   Rothman, Benny, *The 1932 Kinder Trespass.* p. 45
14   *Rucksack* Vol. 10, No.8. June 1982
15   Stephenson, Tom, *Forbidden Land,* p 163
16   Hill, Howard, *The Freedom to Roam – The Struggle for Access to*
    Britain's Moors and Mountains. Moorland Publishing, Ashbourne, 1980
    pp 70, 73
17   Ibid. 76, 77
18   *The Manchester Guardian,* 1st July 1935
19   *Keep Out.* The Ramblers' Association, London 1984. pp 8-10
20   *The Ramblers' Yearbook, 1928.* pp 15,16
21   *Liverpool Post and Mercury,* June 25th, 1928
22   Ibid.
23   *National Parks and Access to the Countryside Bill (Second Reading)*
    31st March 1949 Hansard – Fifth Series Vol. 463 Col 1461

INDEX

Abbey Brook Access Rally, 193
Access Bill, 1939, 67.193
Access Bills, various, 198
Access to Mountains, Scotland Bill, 55
Allerdice, Robert Barclay – "Captain Barclay" 107
Alpine Club, 74.94
Ashbrook, Kate, 62. 72
'As-You-Like it-Club', 144
Atholl, Duke of, 1-15
Atholl Passport Office, 9

Baker, Dr. E.A. 95
Barnes, Phil. 197
Baron, Barclay, 169
Ben Nevis, ascent of, 20.22
Bethesda Slate Quarry, 100-102
Birkenhead Photographic Society, 88.89
Birkenhead Rover Troop, 145
Blair, Andrew, 200
Blatchford, Robert Glanville, 98-102
British Empire Naturalists' League, 137
British Federation of Youth, 164
British Workers Sports Federation, 182-193
British Youth Council, 164
Brompton, great walk at, 108.109
Brown, "Blower" 109.110
Bryce, James, 49-60. 74. 81
Bryce, Mount, 52
Burnham Beeches, 71
Butler, Arthur John, 78.79
Butlin, Billy, Land's End Walk, 115

Cairngorm Club, 52.56. 92
Carnegie Trust, 168
Chartists, 24

Chubb, Sir Lawrence Wensley, 61.65.67. 142.189. 195
Chums Rambling Group, 137
Clarion, Socialist paper, 99-101
Commons Preservation Society, 61-72. 95.
Corkey, W. 109.110
Council for the Protection of Rural England, 197.
Countryside and Rights of Way Act,2000, 200
Countryside, the Leaving of, 84-86
Crofters Act, 47
Crofters in combat with police, 46
Crofton Park Ramblers, 137

Darwin, Charles, 78
Dear Stalking, 5
Diana, Princess of Wales, 70

Edge, Joseph, 108
Ellis, Tom, MP, 56.57
Embledon, A, 165
Epping Forest, 62.64
Equestrians v Pedestrians, 139
Eversley, Baron, 61.70

Fairclough, T.F. 165
Federation of Rambling Clubs, 170
Foot Travellers' Song, 141,142
Forest Ramblers' Club, 89.90
Foster Powell, 106-107

Gale, William, 108
Galton, Francis, 74
German Youth Hostels, 163.164
German Youth Movement, 160-165
Gipsy Journal and British Tourist, 90
Glasgow, living conditions, 15
Glen Tilt, 1-15

Goebbels, Dr., 167

Hampstead Heath, 62.63
Harrington Conservatives Al-Frescoes Group, 137

Heathen Rambling Club, 137
Highbury United Rambling Club, 137
Highland Clearances, 11.14
Highlands, tourists to, 15.16. 17-27
Hiking Boom, 1930's, 160
Hill, Howard, 62
Hill, Octavia, 65.66. 69
Hitler, Adolf, 164. 167.168.
Holt Hostel, Maeshafn, 166
Holt, Lawrence, 166
Hop Pickers, 91.92
Hunter, Sir Robert, 61, 64

Joad, Dr. Cyril Edward Murchison, 197.
Johnson, Sir John (LDWA) 117
Jones, Arthur Creech, 198

Kinder Scout Mass Trespass, 182-193
Kintail shooting estate 31-45
Kleist, Bernd, Heinrich von, 161.162
Kyndwr Club, 95

Lake District and the 'Lakers' 118-131
Liverpool Botanical Society, 145
Liverpool, 'Capital of Wales', 144
Liverpool District Ramblers' Federation, 144. 164. 165
Liverpool Fabian Society, 145
Liverpool Y.M.C.A. Ramblers, 87.88
Long Distance Walkers, 106-117
Long Distance Walkers' Association: A Brief History of, 115-117

Macdonald, Hugh, 23-26
Macrae, Murdo, 28-48

Manchester and District Ramblers' Federation, 189.193.
Manchester Pedestrian Club, 135.136
'Manchester Rambler', the, 193
Manchester Ramblers' Council, 170
Manchester Rucksack Club, 132.134
Manchester - Southport Walk of 1903, 114.115
McColl, Ewan, 193.
Meredith, George, 78
Merseyside's Mountains, 144
Midges, battle of, 36.37
Mill, John Stuart, 61
Mitchell, George. 195.
Moore, Dr. Barbara, 115

National Council of Ramblers' Federations – become the Ramblers' Association in 1935, 173
National Trust, 197
Northumbrian Trampers' Guild, 160

Otten, Karl, 161

Peak Districk and Northern Counties Footpaths Preservation Society, 171
Pennine Way, 177-181.195.196
Penrhyn, Lord, 100-102
Pioneer Rambling clubs, 1874-1900, 84-97
Pioneer Rambling Clubs, early 20th Century, 132-147
Pollack, Sir Frederick, 77. 81

Ramblers' Association, establishment of, 170-181.198.199
Ramblers, Federations, 1930's, 172.173
'Ramblers Parliament', (Hope) 170
Ranken Rambling Club, 137
Rawnsley, Canon, 65
Robertson, George Croom, 76

'Romanticism', 161
Rothman, Bernard, 182-193
Rucksack Club, 95
Ruskin, John, 69-70

Schirrman, Richard, 164
Scout Jamboree, Birkenhead, 165
Sheffield and District Ramblers'
Federation, 170.196.
Sheffield Clarion Ramblers, 98-105
Silkin, Lewis, 100
Smith, Brian, (LDWA) 116
"Socialist, how to make a", 202
Speedwell Ramblers, 144
Spencer, Earl, 70
Stephens, Leslie, 54. 61. 73-83
Stephenson, Tom, 66. 172. 175-181.
193.
'Strength through Joy' 167
Sunday Tramps, 54. 73-83

Thurstaston Hill Access Rallies,
199.200
Trespassers will be prosecuted, 68

Vegetarian Cycling and Athletic Club,
145
Vegetarian, thousand mile walk of a,
113.114
Vermin, 1

Walking Tours, incidents on, 143
Wallasey Amateur Photographic
Society, 145
Wallasey Independent Labour Party,
145. 146
Wallasey Rambling Club, 146
Wandervogel, 162-164
Ward, G.B.H. 98. 103-105.194. 198.
Wessex Hikers' Lodges, 160
West of Scotland Ramblers'
Federation. 26.170

Weston's Great Temperance Walk,
111-112
Whymper, Edward, 74. 82.83. 94
Williams, Sir George (Y.M.C.A.) 87
Wimbledon Common, 70   W
Winans, W.L. 28-48
Winnats Pass Access Rallies, 192.
196-199
Wirral Group, Ramblers' Association,
146
Wirral Ramblers, Wallasey, 1927, 146

Y.M.C.A. 87.88
Yorkshire Ramblers' Club, 92-97
Young Naturalist's League, 136
Youth Hostel Association, 160-169